The Wherewithal

The Wherewithal

A Novel in Verse

Philip Schultz

W. W. NORTON & COMPANY

NEW YORK | LONDON

Manufacturing by Courier Westford
Book design by Fearn Cutler de Vicq
Production manager: Devon Zahn

ISBN 978-0-393-24094-8

W. W. Norton & Company, Inc.
500 Fifth Avenue, New York, N.Y. 10110
www.wwnorton.com

W. W. Norton & Company Ltd.
Castle House, 75/76 Wells Street, London W1T 3QT

1 2 3 4 5 6 7 8 9 0

for Drenka Willen

When finding, as in this case, animals which seem to play so insignificant a part in the great scheme of nature, one is apt to wonder why they were created. But it should always be recollected, that in some other country perhaps they are essential members of society, or at some former period may have been so.

—CHARLES DARWIN

Jews who found themselves in DP camps in Germany after the war—as we know, some 200,000 Jews fled from Poland after 1945, mostly to these camps—used to say that Germans would never forgive the Jews for what they had done to them.

—JAN T. GROSS

Henry Jekyll stood at times aghast before the acts of Edward Hyde; but the situation was apart from ordinary laws, and insidiously relaxed the grasp of conscience. It was Hyde, after all, that was guilty.

—ROBERT LOUIS STEVENSON

Despite my alienation from myself at that moment, and though I was nothing but a battleground for invisible forces, I was aware of every detail of what was going on around me.

—KNUT HAMSUN

The Wherewithal

ONE

Henryk Stanislaw Wyrzykowski confesses:

How I Became Head Clerk of Closed Files,

Department of One

1

Upstairs,
it's San Francisco 1968 April 17
and every day the world spins faster on its axis,
a little more off-kilter,
a little less in its right mind,
bursting at its seams with desire for variation,
while everyone everywhere around me
appears to be fornicating
in doorways and on rooftops,
in spiraling parks under transplanted palms
beside rhododendron beds,
marching and waving fists
in wheels of sweltering air,
hurrying in every direction
possessed of an overflowing innocence
and furious resolve
and revolutionary zeal—indeed—
hurling themselves
against barricades of forlorn ideals
and ancient decrees,
throwing off rusty shadows
and leafy inane inner beings,
singing unholy penitential psalms
full of righteous sorrow . . . yes,
forgiving nothing
while remembering everything . . .
while I, one

Henryk Stanislaw Wyrzykowski,
Head Clerk of Closed Files,
a department of one,
work,
for the time being,
in a hole in the earth
hiding from the US Army,
from a vast personal history
of defeat and occupation,
of anger and despair,
among other things,

work,
in a forgotten well of ghostly sighs,
where, more often than not,
it's Poland 1941 June 25
and in the town of Jedwabne
a great massacre is taking place
and the world has stopped in its tracks.

2

I wish I could say I possessed the wherewithal
(like Ludwig Wittgenstein) to regard
my thoughts as mere remarks
that can be condoned and trusted,
rather than footnotes,
or facsimiles of actual thoughts,

which when pushed
"against their own inclination"
become the scattered dependents
of an orphaned mind,
who, basically,
want nothing more to do with me.

In other words,
despite enjoying a mere half-life—
no wife, girlfriend, family or friends—
I remain (to myself at least)
somewhat "interesting,"
more than a quickly passing blur
blending lizard-like into the gray air
as I sneak down hallways,
hiding in the frayed inside pocket
of a nervous suit jacket,
my wallet and keys,
avoiding those whom only recently
I was counted among,
the odious odiferous crowding the halls,
offices and urine-stained lobbies
of this mercy depot,
this fortress of dolor,
whom I'm now employed to serve,
and who therefore see me
for what I am—guardian of nobody,
solicitor of nothing,
unnatural ferryman lugging a cargo
of dissolute souls

from one hostile shore to another
for no reason other than
to sustain myself to the next paycheck . . .

3

Leaning all the way back
in a swivel chair, cradling my aching head,
my recycled cowboy boots crossed
on a small mountain of files assigned
for further procrastination,
further dubiousness,
in a clearing wide enough for a desk,
two chairs, a rancid water cooler,
four phones, three battered filing cabinets,
a splintered two-fanged coatrack,
and a poorly framed etching
of the spectacular dungeon gloom
of Giovanni Battista Piranesi's *Carcere,*
with Arches and Pulleys
and a Smoking Fire in the Center,
nailed to a cinderblock wall,
all of which now is swaying
under the cracked illumination
of a dusty street window
that permits a paltry sliver view
of mostly fancy shoes heading west
along Bush Street in posh downtown San Francisco,

not to mention, ten hissing fluorescent lamps
clinging to angry ceiling shadows
like metallic arachnids casting
a sulfuric gloom over a forest
of 1,000 sq. miles of floor-to-ceiling
metal shelves stuffed to bursting
with 700,640 inactive files
recording every sort of grievance,
indignity and plea for sustenance
suffered in the Bay Area between
September 23,1968 and July 15, 1959
when such documentation was first evaluated,
filed, and quickly forgotten
in this branch of
the California Department of Social Services,
in whose bomb shelter of a basement
I now sit snug as a bug,
my pulse a strong breeze,
a steady 15 knots
on the Beaufort Wind Scale.

4

One year younger than I,
Rossy,
a seventeen-year-old Polish American Jew,
who never played chicken before,
bought a .22 rifle to shoot pigeons

and a few confused rats
in the old railroad yards
on the outside of the dark inside of North Chicago,
with a fake driver's license and a hubris
first inspired,
and then deflated by me.

Rossy,
who lived eight houses down
on the other side of a street filled
with obsolete refugees
and antique trees,
wore patched black chinos,
white shirts with upturned collars,
stuttered every third word
and ran with elbows aloft like chicken wings,
because I did, stood glistening
in a field of high grass,
behind mounds of rusted tracks,
joking around with me
while provoking it seemed
an investigation into something
that seemed to require
a somewhat perverse curiosity
and resigned belief
in the intangible ecstasy of violence.

Seventeen
nevertheless

is old enough to understand
that death isn't a game.

But
what was it then?

Well,
it was July, late morning,
humid and slow,
a cloudless, stagnant sky.
No wind to speak of,
not a wing to be seen.

The beginning and end
of any meaning I'd ever own.

5

Like my predecessor,
Arthur P. Swigge,
I gauge the stormy vacillations
of my emotional states
on the Beautfort Wind Scale,
which is taped to a shelf above my desk,
a red circle around *strong breeze*
with the word *trouble* scrawled over it;
over Force No.: *pulse readings*:

Beaufort Force No.	State of Air	Wind Velocity in Knots
0	calm	0–1
1	light airs	1–3
2	slight breeze	4–6
3	gentle breeze	7–10
4	moderate breeze	11–16
5	fresh breeze	17–21
6	strong breeze	22–27
7	moderate gale	28–33
8	fresh gale	34–40
9	strong gale	41–47
10	whole gale	48–55
11	storm	56–65
12	hurricane	above 65

Swigge,
famous for his collections
of lesbian pornography, ceramic turtles,
vintage baseball cards,
and various arcane specimens
of pharmaceutical nirvana,
left six densely impacted notepads
entitled: Notes of a Know Nothing
filled with crotchety complaints
about other staff members,
and dyspeptic political commentary
locked (I broke in) in a desk drawer,
was found crouched (and filed correctly)
in the S section of Home Relief (for non-veterans),
O.D. on heroin, his large hands cupping

his equally large leafy ears,
his mouth opened wide, as if still emitting
a howl so persuasive it registered a storm
of hurricane velocity, thus achieving
the act the Mick Jagger quote
framed on his desk suggests:
the only performance that makes it . . .
makes it all the way . . . is the one
that achieves madness.

6

If necessary,
I could blame Thanksgiving,
 or Aristotle, or graduate school in the Midwest,
or my believing I was being invited
to dinner at my chairman's house
because I had nowhere else to go.
Thinking his charity elastic,
I invited five others. His peeved look
said it wasn't. An Aristotelian,
he considered Ludwig Wittgenstein,
the subject of my thesis,
a cranky, dangerous mystic.
An argument I assumed is what he wanted.
Ludwig, I'd explain, was an interpretative
and analytic oddball, a seeker
of the linguistic sublime,

but inside the byzantine and musical spheres
of his thought transcendence surged.
But unlike his master
the Chairman's interest in relationships
was limited to me and his wife,
whom he was leaving for his secretary.

Everyone,
as Aristotle might've put it,
wished to exist in any state
other than where
and what he was.

7

If of a mind to
one might ask:
Why is he down here?

Because
by waiting in the wrong line
for bus fare and food stamps
he overheard clerks discussing
finding someone dumb enough to work
in "absolute isolation for very little pay . . ."
and, in the lobby men's toilet,
after quickly wetting colicky hair
and licking at a moustache designed

to hide a cleft palate, he became,
magically it seemed,
the new Closed Files Clerk,
and vanished (by dropping a single *z*)
inside the sober anonymity
of his last name, thereby escaping
his draft board's ferocious reach?

For the solitude with which to translate
into English his mother's Jedwabne diaries
which in fearsome detail describes
the pitchforking, raping, clubbing
and stabbing to death of 1,600 Jewish men,
women and children by their Polish neighbors,
and thereby begin to understand
where she found the wherewithal
to hide seven Jews in a hole in the ground
under our barn for two and a half years,
where animals ate and defecated
and Germans came with dogs
and our neighbors with pitchforks and clubs
to kill witnesses to their slaughter?

Because
every detail of the October Sunday afternoon
when he placed on the dreamy head
of his best and only friend
a Campbell's mushroom soup can
and fired a .22 caliber bullet
directly into the epicenter of his forehead,

an inch below his hairline,
refuses to stop roiling about
inside the pitiless turbine
of his thoughts?

Let us simply say:
all of the above.

8

In Amsterdam
Anne Frank's museum is permanently sanctified.
In Jerusalem's Yad Vashem
Mother's enshrined as Righteous Among Nations.
Outside of Chicago she now sits
rocking in an Alzheimer's ward,
trying to remember her name,
the date and time. Anne Frank moved
from Frankfurt to Amsterdam
to Auschwitz to Bergen-Belsen
to the Hereafter, a Jewish Christ,
sanctified by victimhood.

Ludwig Wittgenstein,
who moved from Vienna to Cambridge, England,
to a prison camp in Italy to a house
in rural Norway to die of cancer,
was enshrined in an idea

that thoughts were pictures
and pictures a model of reality, said:
"I don't know my way about . . . and hence
the aim of philosophy is to shew
the fly out of the fly-bottle."

In an attempt to find our way about,
we moved, mostly in the dark of night,
from Jedwabne to other Polish towns,
and finally to Chicago where,
after killing Rossy, I zigzagged all the way
to this hole in the earth
as deep and dark as the one
under our barn,
only to arrive, one could claim,
where I started from.

9

Upstairs,
when someone waiting in line for,
say, bus fare, begins weeping
someone else begins laughing,
when someone hauls off and hits someone,
someone else steps back, as if struck,
when someone begins eating,
say, a pork chop, someone else
licks his chops, dreaming of banquets,

when someone preparing himself
to be assessed loses all hope,
someone else (perhaps a social worker,
a bureaucrat) Capitalizes his thoughts,
speaks the language of chronology,
pictures, times and dates,
the language of exclamation points,
insidious signs and nomenclature
posted everywhere in the halls upstairs:

> IT'S YOUR RESPONSIBILITY!
> TO PICK UP YOUR FOOD STAMPS!
> FOLLOW THESE RULES REGARDING
> YOUR IDENTIFICATION CARD!
> GET AN APPLICATION
> WHEN YOU ASK FOR ONE!
> IF YOU TELL US TODAY
> THAT YOU HAVE AN *EMERGENCY!*
> WE MUST INTERVIEW YOU TODAY!
> ABOUT YOUR *EMERGENCY!*
> OR YOU COULD LOSE
> YOUR PUBLIC ASSISTANCE!
> MEDICAL ASSISTANCE!
> RENT ALLOWANCE BUS FARE!
> CHILD AND SPOUSAL SUPPORT!

Upstairs
when someone for any reason is unable
to state his particular reasons for existing,
or stake a position, say,

on the United States vs. Vietnam
youthful enthusiasm vs. boredom
scathing denunciation vs. racist exploitation
the dollar-for-dollar precipitous decline
of all sympathy and mercy . . .
someone else gives up seeking
the difference between things
that could've been
and weren't
and things that didn't have to be
but were.

Upstairs,
as Swigge's notebooks repeatedly point out,
everyone is dependent on everyone else,
and therefore, desperately,
obviously, inescapably
despises everyone else.

10

After Thanksgiving,
but before the Chairman left his wife,
after I was invited to every dinner
with visiting VIPs, but before
everyone started whispering
and staring at me in bars and movie houses,
when I became an impertinent curiosity

fearful of running away and
losing my draft deferment,
I went to his office to plead my innocence,
which is when he said,
"I hear you're good to talk to,
well, I like talking."

After he began driving me
around the frozen farmland
in his ratty old Jeep, screaming
over the wind rattle, "Every
important philosopher was Greek,
Roman or Presbyterian,
maybe Methodist, but,
except for Spinoza, never Jewish—
stop wasting your time on Wittgenstein!"
and before I moved into his farmhouse
with his wife and two daughters
and he into my room in town,
each morning I'd wake to see
his wife, Betty, perched
at the far end of my bed,
a ravishing flamingo, cooing,
"Darling, you're the love of my life."

Mother,
the daughter of farmers,
said she memorized the Old Testament
in order to think like a Jew
and thereby rid herself of original sin.
There was nothing original, she believed,
about owning someone else's sin.

She claimed she understood
why her neighbors killed all their Jews.
Not only for their property
(which they took), or because
they'd collaborated with the Bolsheviks,
(in order to survive, everyone did),
or were communists (whose ideology
hated everyone equally),
or because they envied them
(they envied everyone),
or because, in order to survive,
someone had to be
one ladder rung lower than
their opinion of themselves.

No,
her neighbors killed and kept on killing Jews,
because the Jews knew
what they had done to them.
Knew who and what they were.

After being struck,
Rossy's stare continued to express incredulity—
had I actually killed him, I,
whom in every way he tried to emulate?

Never before was perfection within his reach.
But now, after the shot echoed
and the sky flattened and swallowed itself,
he continued to stand upright,
the clean, now unlikely-
ever-to-be-opened soup can
still balanced on the crown of his head,
he seemed pleased
with the notion that equilibrium
had been reached,
one situated perfectly
between
nothing and nowhere.

Realizing this,
I screamed for him to please duck.

Indeed,
Mother and I both have our Jews.
Hers the seven she saved.

Mine these disaffected ghettoized facts and footnotes,
these sad angry prodigies of distraught humanity,
these savage facsimiles waiting in line
to be herded somewhere else,
according to laws and codes
they can't understand, rendered
for millennia beside the point,
these human stand-ins
entombed in ironic obsolescence,
not to mention those whom,
deep in the middle of winter nights,
I actually fed, gave blankets to against the wind,
warned to hide in the woods,
was beaten and called "Jew"
by my classmates because of,
those whom Mother loved more,
and I therefore hated, envied
and admired, and one day,
in the streets of my birthplace
watched being herded into Sleszynski's barn,
where, doused with kerosene and lit
like sacrificial figurines
screamed and screamed
and screamed.

Believe me,
I know Jews.

I don't know myself
but I know Jews.

14

Is irony the right word to describe
how Mother's Alzheimer's erased
the part of her life she wanted to remember
and rendered vividly the part
she wanted to forget?
Is it merely one of Ludwig's
perverse paradoxes?

In any case, every detail
of Mother and I holding hands
on a teak bench in a tiny park
outside the ivy-covered brick building
on the outskirts of Chicago
a little over a year ago, is limned
in my memory, even the women's names
on the brass tree plaques (mothers,
I'd think, Beth Mary Bev Delores),
her right hand beautifully fitted
into my left, each of her knuckles
and stamp like fingertips achieving
the same feeling of inevitability.

Only yesterday these fingers
pushed hair from my eyes
and pointed to the barn behind our house,
and then beyond to the woods,
knowing I'd know
the "signal" being given?

Her blue eyes focused inward,
as if no longer interested in the outside,
as if having forgotten that their purpose
was to recognize
and name
and memorialize
and not erase.

15

Her diaries begin on July 10, 1941,
the day the non-Jewish half
of Jedwabne's population attacked
and murdered the Jewish half,
and end on January 15, 1949,
a year after she arrived in Chicago.
Because I'm not a translator or scholar
and her lack of education,
and bad grammar requires
clarification and notation,
I chose not to correct or explain
the unexplainable, wanting
the astonishment of her own words.

Numbered 7 to 22, six are missing.
Hidden under her bedroom closet floorboards,
number 7 begins:

Who didn't know what was happening?
My husband Andrzej knew, my son Henryk
and daughter Krystyna were little but they knew—
everybody knew. First the Russian monsters, then
the Nazis. My eyes watched what my neighbors did
to the Jews from the June day in 1941 when
the Germans came and the pogrom started with
the Borowski brothers going door to door, playing
an accordion so no one would hear the screams—
who did they think would hear—God?—stoning
with bricks, plucking old man Krawiecki's eyes out
cutting off his tongue, everyone pretending only
the Germans did such things . . . not us who sold them
cows tipped our hats good morning we wouldn't kill
and torture people we knew since we were children . . .

why . . . because they had better houses clothes shops
worked harder had more faith . . . cheering an old man
crying for mercy without a tongue . . .

sitting and clapping on the banks of the pond
as sweet young Chaja Kubrzanska and her best friend
Basia Binsztajn whom I knew since they were infants
tried to drown their newborns rather than let them
be ripped apart . . . everyone laughing and giving advice
on how best to drown an infant . . . my neighbors mothers
and fathers so proud of themselves . . . imagine holding
your newborn under water . . . the strength and love it takes . . .
the faith that God would love them now . . .

and not a German in sight . . .

Loitering upstairs,
these curious specimens,
asleep on their feet,
staring into barred windows,
drinking out of bags
the elixir nothingness—

might one ask: who they are?

Their tortured argot,
aborted attempts to determine
what is owed them by fate?

We are the carpet under which
their vagueness is swept,
the means by which the forlorn ugliness
of their gaze is rendered inconspicuous.

Angst-ridden, befuddled,
each a decapitated fugue,
a broken contract,
an inventory of neglect,
an invisible witness,
a peculiar hiccup, an out-of-sync
factory of relentless complaint,
in which Swigge and now I
are collaborators, cogs, weak links
and amanuenses attempting,

however dubiously,
to define and explain how
and why they should be classified,
verified, terminated
and further vilified.

Henryk Stanislaw Wyrzykowski gets a job:

How I Went from Barely Existing on Public

Assistance

to Being Down Here,

Among These Ghostly Sighs

I

Because 1-A's could be called up the next day,
no one was hiring me,
so I'd go to the docks,
work maybe one day in six,
and then try Yellow, where Ruby,
the epically obscene dispatcher,
liked to ask why
a long-haired radical fuckface shirker like me
wasn't out killing gooks in Nam, goddamnit!
I got by on food stamps, stealing rib eyes
from the IGA, a bizarre and noisy solitude,
some thirty-three varieties of philosophical
and sexual melancholy, not to mention
being sequestered within a decade
indelibly stained with curious appetites.
I didn't own a TV, was too busy evading
the US Army to read newspapers,
but I'd seen the Zodiac's coded communiqués
and crazy cryptograms, bragging
how much fun killing human beings was,
that thus far his inventory included:
four men, three women, a cop
and maybe some thirty-seven other innocents.

So one cloudy Monday morning
after the night the maniac told
the *San Francisco Chronicle*

he'd kill a cabbie next
I showed up at Yellow Cab
knowing only that I was hungry,
and looking around the empty locker room,
I asked Ruby why
he was finally hiring me.
"Must be your lucky day, shithead," he said.

2

Yes,
drop from your last name
one measly little letter,
change your middle initial,
grow the kind of moustache favored
by overzealous Russian revolutionaries
and,
as far as the US Army cares,
you've disappeared into the woeful alphabet
of the comatose, the spent
and the gone-away-somewhere,
because basically, "who'd lie about
being named Henryk P. Wyrzykowski?"

Which is why
upon seeing
my new dungeon paradise,
I gasped in utter elation.

3

Rossy's father survived Treblinka,
but not this. Each night
his shiny black Cadillac roared past our house
screaming "Nazi murderer!"
Unconvincingly, Mother thought,
his hatred sounding all used up.

Meanwhile,
everyone but I agreed
it was an accident—no one
kills someone he loves.
After being tried and found innocent,
and placed under observation,
without graduating high school,
or owning any understanding
of how to proceed,
I left Chicago.

Thereafter,
upon seeing me,
my mother averted her eyes.

Her violet eyes
never again valued me.

4

Meanwhile,
the Chairman and I continued driving
around the far-flung mostly frozen farmland,
I listening (kind of) to his endless monologue
festooned with quotes from Heidegger,
"The true is what corresponds to the real,
and the real is what is in truth,"
he'd shout gleefully, meaning:
I shouldn't feel guilty,
I wasn't stealing his wife,
I was providing her with a quality
valued above all others by Aristotle,
a sympathetic ear.

Yes,
but Aristotle also liked swapping identities,
exchanging one day for the next,
the one for the many,
Eternal Things for Perishable Ones.
Man being what comes from man
but a bed not from another bed,
thus: "It is not the shape
but the wood that is the bed's nature."

Therein,
it was in my nature to inherit
not only his farmhouse,
and the attention of a highly regarded
department of philosophy,

but both the nature
and shape of *his* bed,
each real and therefore true enough.

5

On my way this morning
to Central Index to verify the forfeiture
of further state responsibility
to a certain Joseph Fisk, whose
Aid to Victims of Crimes of Violence
ended yesterday in a Mission District alleyway,
where his body was found, skull split open,
a pamphlet is handed to me
by someone draped in soiled sheets,
who sprinkles urine in my face, saying,
"Your soul, have you checked the wiring lately?"

Ampère's Law: "that a magnetic field induced by
an electrical current directly proportional to the product
of the current intensity and the length of the conductor,
inversely proportional to the square of the distance
between point and conductor, and perpendicular to
the plane joining them." A.M. Ampère, Esq. In God We Trust.

Yesterday,
Joseph Fisk was a born victim,
his worker noted, an ex-Marine/bank clerk,
one of nine kids abandoned to foster homes,

eleven arrests for assault, panhandling,
breaking and entering drugstores,
robbed, beaten, and molested forty-two times
by the age of sixteen—today,
facts to be verified, a file to be closed
indefinitely. One might ask:
Who cares?

The city and state do, Swigge believed,
only if his case,
and therefore existence,
is active, our goal here
being "to withhold as much
from as many
for as long as possible."

Ludwig said: "I tell someone I am in pain.
His attitude to me will then be that of belief;
disbelief; suspicion; and so on."

In other words,
it's not our job to ask
how much pain a soul can bear
but to gauge the distance
between what Mr. Ampère would describe
as the square of the distance
between point and conductor,
between one's current, or life force,
and the intensity of the pain
of one's belief in the hereafter.

To check the wiring
of the perpendicular and the prostrate,
the inverse and the proportional,
the soiled and the induced,
the sprinkler and the sprinkled-upon,
not to mention,
the living and the dead.

6

A drunken, sphinx-faced ophthalmologist
from Toledo, my third and last ride,
waited hours for a ride,
because mine, he said, was maybe
the only cab in the Bay Area.
I was too busy making money to notice, I said,
"Well, either you own Paul Bunyan's balls,
Houdini's death wish, or are just plain fucking stupid—
for all you know I'm the Zodiac!"

Unfolding his Chronicle, he read the headline:
" 'Zodiac promises to kill a cabbie next!'
In Toledo we know when to be scared shitless!"

Time slowed to a one-car funeral procession.
On every corner people clapped, waved,
shouted advice, and weighed my chances.
Too scared to stop, I zigzagged, circled
and crisscrossed a steaming marsh

(the river Styx?) hitherto and wayward
without stopping for lights, urination,
 coffee, or breath, forwards and backwards
without subtlety, faith, God or grammar,
collectively and en masse, bouncing
and bursting like a prayer a goat a train
 a grounded plane a beast on all fours
expecting a bullet in its brain,
while everything outside my foggy windows
appeared forbidden,
forlorn and frightened—

on the lam again, chased by
a poisonous hodgepodge of blasphemous
and impetuous ideology,
apparently, the Viet Cong,
the US government, uninterrupted
flocks of a withering bourgeoisie,
and now this Zodiac maniac
all wanting only one thing,

all the while
the ophthalmologist
and Ruby screamed a dour duet,
"A hundred bucks to let me out, two hundred!"
"Motherfucker, pick somebody up!"

7

Unlike Auschwitz or Birkenau,
which endorsed the illusion of a workplace,
Treblinka, a train platform
and a one-way road to eternity,
was a place, Rossy's father told Rossy,
where illusion didn't exist,
just corpses burning all night on grills,
greasing the sky with an effluvium
medieval in its spite, inspired perhaps
by the unspent imaginations of generations,
where a lucky few survived by pulling
precious gems from the teeth of the dead
and cut and swept miles and miles
of women's hair, which, as a history
of brushings and intimate caresses,
were stored faithfully in woven baskets
in the Survivor's dreams.

At night he covered with sand
the bodypits which turned red
in the morning light. Once or twice
a hand or foot twitched on the surface,
indicating perhaps what
the Dead Sea Scrolls prophesized,
that the final war between those
of heightened purity and those
who "walk in the wicked way"
had arrived.

On a garage shelf under which
on a tiny army cot the Survivor slept
boxes were labeled:
Rossy's black curls at 19 wks,
at 53 mns, at year 8, etc.
hair cut over Rossy's protests of course.

The day after I killed his son,
the fires of Treblinka
were turned on me.

8

"What does it mean to know *who* is in pain?"
Ludwig asked himself.
What criteria determines what can be tolerated
in any one place and time?

For instance: every morning and night
I saw three cots side by side inside the hole
upon which seven people slept
back to back, face to face,
elbow against knee, arms folded,
hands embraced, noses pressed
against cheeks, a falling mist
of crumbling dirt, dreams divided and spread out
over vast fields of sky and wind,
overlapping, naked and rotting,

flame-encrusted, smelling of lice-infected feet,
snores echoing as if enclosed
permanently inside ghostly sighs . . .

9

Upstairs,
each department owns its own number
of dedicated bell rings,
because it's believed
all male staff must run lickety-split to trouble,
always be present at the apocalypse,
at least that's what Lou Phillips in personnel
believes, having learned this system
aboard a WWII destroyer, which is why
he's hated by every man who works here,
especially Swigge and me.

About Lou Swigge wrote: "Brags he's fucked
every girl in the 3rd floor typing pool, gels his hair
to fall seductively over his Mt. Rushmore forehead,
exhales bourbon, sighs atonally speaks haltingly
to assure staunch attention, adores recordings
of whales mating, once knocked a drunken
Sioux Indian, on his hands and knees, looking
for a dislodged glass eye, down the back stairs,
claiming the man tripped him, often makes late

night phone calls to recite his putrid poetry to
female staff he hired . . .

"Upstairs, it's 18th century England, where
farming out the poor meant lumping the blind,
crippled, insane, epileptic, deaf and dumb
in almshouses with criminals because The History
of the Poor Laws was designed to discourage mendacity,
wherein anyone giving alms to beggars was put in jail . . ."

In other words,
little has changed—many still believed
there's no distinction
between tolerating
the suffering of others
and causing it.

10

Rossy couldn't pass his driver's test,
return a library book, memorize anything.
He took art classes when I became
the high school cartoonist, bought
three plaid shirts when I bought one,
and when I didn't let him tag along
on my movie dates he'd sit alone
in the balcony, three rows back,
eating popcorn and weeping.

And when I asked him to,
he placed a soup can on his head
and stood there, smiling at me.

II

Down here,
strolling this redundant orchard,
for no particular reason I'll pluck
a plump file and read aloud:
Gertrude Forrio: barmaid, mother of three,
on AFDC, married twice, three
prostitution arrests; two suicide attempts;
addicted to diamorphine diacetylmorphine
(heroin); death due, after losing
a waitressing job, to self-asphyxiation
with a plastic laundry bag; diagnoses:
low self-esteem and depression due
to parental neglect, learning disabilities,
HS dropout, high metabolism, physical,
emotional and spiritual exhaustion.

Down here,
hidden from the world above,
wallowing in a phantasmagoria of wounds,
insults, silent and grotesque,
the Fisks and Forrios, lost
in an infinite forest of inhospitable
and ghostly echoes,

where I too find myself
alone
at the intersection of luck and disgrace,
waiting indefinitely
for a light to change.

12

One hapless Tuesday morning,
her big blue dilated eyes startled
to find me in Swigge's chair,
a tall, fetchingly beleaguered,
young familiar-looking blond woman
in a cowhide miniskirt and billowy
peasant blouse, appears
out of the fluorescent haze,
asking, "Swigge, he still work here?"

"He's dead, gone, missing and/or deceased," I say.
"Well, we, kind of . . . had an arrangement."

Which was, she said:
In return for PA extensions
(which Swigge delivered, he wrote
in his notebooks, by ghostwriting love letters
for Mrs. Cafiso in Central Index
to a Stevie Boy in Maintenance),

she posed for him, sometimes with a girlfriend,
it being what he wanted—
was there something I wanted?
"You don't like photos there's other things."

After leaving her case number and phone number,
she disappeared magnificently
into the same shadows she'd appeared
out of only moments before.

Under his Tijuana Gold, much-tampered
with paper clips, neatly dated and immaculately
written notepads in Swigge's bottom drawer,
I find files labeled: *For Mine Eyes Only!*
in which one is entitled: "Heddie Butterfly:
22 yrs old, 18 months on PA, 10 extended
psychiatric visits, youngest of eight
father-abandoned kids from Big Sky, Montana,
mother-committed to a Seattle psych ward,
father in prison, part-time go-go girl,
two arrests for drug dealing, three abortions
paid by us, one and a half suicide attempts,"
along with fifteen photos of her and another girl,
posing, let us say, somewhat provocatively,
which is why she looks so familiar.

One and a half suicide attempts?
My pulse 21 knots, a very ungentle breeze.

13

Hitting empty
sometime past midnight,
I parked on a cliff overlooking
the fog-encrusted imperiousness
of the Pacific Ocean, where,
I read somewhere, 80 percent of us prefer to live,
at the edge, at or near the beginning
or end of things, away from
the cluttered middle, where
none of the action is.

Then, awakened
at four in the morning
by my radio screeching a cabbie
was found in the Oakland Hills,
shot straight through the back of his head,
I finally understood such sundry vulgarities
as the Tet Offensive, Sleszynski's barn,
and the inevitability in Rossy's eyes,
all the while Ruby screaming,
"I just wish it was you, shithead!"

14

To try to imagine someone else's pain
using your own as a model
is misleading, Ludwig suggests.
Such a transition isn't practical,
or even possible. Perhaps this is why
workers here are trained not to see
the surrounding pain, to shut out all sensation
and focus on the ever-flowering minutiae
of the case at hand. Pain isn't a "description
of a mental state" but a "signal"
or metaphor for sensation. Because,
Ludwig says, the real subject of pain
is the suffering that gives it expression.

Is empathy therefore an illusion?
Is there no grief but our own?
Potentially are we all monsters?

1) What if memory C were collapsed into memory H?
2) What criteria would be used to understand
    the language of a thought no one can remember?
3) Yesterday Mother lived in a house on a street
    in a town which all had names—would they
    still exist if their names disappeared?
4) Suppose a picture of an imaginary landscape
    with a young woman sitting on a porch unable
    to remember her desire to enter the house—
    would she be in pain if she couldn't do so?

5) Suppose the present moment as an island
   surrounded by a vast ocean—imagine Jedwabne
   occurring over and over again on the island.
6) If this is a signal what does it signify?

                                            ‡

15

Given its volume and onslaught,
Mother understood it was history
attacking her and attempted to shame it
with its own crimes. Was this the purpose
of her diaries—not to be sacrificed to history?

Booklet number 8 begins:

*. . . from each profession the Gestapo wanted one Jewish family
but Bronislaw Sleszynski argued there were enough Polish
craftsmen and our mayor agreed that not one Jew should
be spared—already in their eyes, the killing and blood,
their hands hanging like clubs . . . people I went to school with
kneeled with each Sunday—strangers whose souls
had been stolen . . .*

*not children but animals to be slaughtered . . . the memory grows
heavier every day . . . until even . . . one's faith dies . . . how could I
be so blind not to see what was coming—Christ died for
these people . . .*

when the first Jews came in the night I took them in and
those afterwards . . . we all dug the hole with shovels, rakes
our own hands . . . I was possessed with God's strength . . . their
eyes full of another world . . . their fear more powerful than
my faith . . . is this what Christ felt on the cross . . . what was in
their eyes . . .

16

"The necessity of providing shelter for those who,
as a result of a catastrophe not of their making,
could no longer provide for themselves the dignity
accorded a human being was easily recognized here,
one would imagine. How, subsequently, those desolate
and penniless flowed from small towns into cities,
where lodgings didn't exist, and thousands without
tangible means wandered aimlessly, entirely without
confidence, or the wherewithal of mortal purpose."

Swigge didn't find this in a statistical report
or social case work, he wrote in his notepads,
but in an article about Jewish life
under German Occupation.

He went on: "In his thesis on Feuerbach,
Karl Marx uses the expression 'dirty Jewish'
to characterize a form of economic behavior:
'Let us consider the real Jew: not the Sabbath Jew . . .

but the everyday Jew. What is the profane basis
of Judaism? Practical need, self-interest.
What is his worldly god? *Money.'*

"Though he came from a family of rabbis,
Marx believed that to be emancipated
from *huckstering* and *money*, from real
and practical Judaism, Jews must cease
to be Jews . . . Must, in fact, cease to be.

"Viewing oneself through the eyes of those
who resent your dependence on them
enables you to see yourself as they do:
a perversion, a bloodthirsty tick,
a venomous parasite, a slap in the face
and burden to all civilized society. Amen!"

In other words,
down here in the catacombs
among these ubiquitous shadows,
in a state of insubstantial,
stalled and undeviating vagueness
maybe I'm also what Mother found
to be most odious: an anti-Semite.

THREE

Henryk Stanislaw Wyrzykowski

awaits

the Furious First Movement

of the Daily Symphony

Two weeks after driving a taxi for one night,
and five months before my job down here,
Giggers Malone, an ex-Marine
under whose right eye an American eagle
tattoo drifted mostly north, hired me,
without asking my draft status
(never a good sign), to fill vending machines
on an aircraft carrier just back
from the Gulf of Tonkin. No training,
not a word about schooling,
work experience, all he said was:
"Fill the fuckers and get the hell out of the way."

So five of us, none of whom appeared
to want to be introduced or know why
guys who knew nothing about vending machines
or aircraft carriers, were hired to do
something this bizarre, parked under
a floating peninsula, helicopters tearing up
the robust northern Californian sky,
cranes swaying off the inflated vanity
of the main deck, sailors running up
and down gangplanks, dangling off scaffolds,
scraping and painting the redoubtable bow
of "the USS *Constellation*, Connie to some"
shouted Giggers, pushing me

out of the way of a forklift.
"These guys get mean waiting on furloughs,
beat the machines up good, insurance
replaces three batches a month,
but destroying machines aint booze and pussy
if you know what I mean. Fifteen minutes
to fill and repair the remains, kiddos!"

2

Mornings I bring coffee
and a cinnamon donut up to
the pigeon-shit gray roof of this scrunched-up,
ill-defined six-story edifice,
which from the street must look
as if it were buckling under the vicissitudes
of a ferocious necessity,
to be astonished
by the robust reach of the fragile sun
and escaping blue-tinged clouds,
under which the eucalyptus/rhododendron mist
drifts
swallowing the big bridge,
and Golden Gate Park
and every office building in downtown San Francisco
in which, in the sun-streaked windows,
a vast army of brisk young women
are diligently *plingaling*

slamming
sharpening
stapling
and affixing objects to various other things
of even more dubious significance,
while, across the street,
a dark-haired sweet-faced gum-chewing honey
is swinging a perfected right ankle
in a slow one-two-one-two-three beat,
churning, you could say,
enough voltage to light every remaining
second Thursday morning in April 1968,
or so it seems,
while below
the ghastly ringing of the 8 a.m. bells
that opens our unwelcoming doors
to the furious first movement
of a quaint heteronymous symphony
that begins the burgeoning
of such disparate variety
of inarticulate need for food, electricity, beauty parlors,
prosthetics, psychiatric scaffolding,
and ill-fitting dentures
Yahweh Himself seems to be roaring:
"You with no hope, Enter!"

3

"In what sort of context does it occur?"
Ludwig said the question was.

In Treblinka, Rossy's father, the Survivor,
said there were bells, shots, meals,
orders and alarms, but no clocks.
Strapped to your wrist
only an unbreakable code
signifying infinity minus one.

A context requires clocks, Ludwig would say.
For something to occur,
something
needed to be lived in, approached,
repelled by, consumed.
The present, to exist,
must be remembered,
despised, and feared.

In other words,
the soup of the past
must contain
the vaguest memory of meat.

In Treblinka,
the Survivor said,
the future ended with the railroad tracks,
promising nothing,

remembering nothing,
not even one's name.

In Treblinka, he said,
the sun was yet to be born.

4

Why,
one might ask, two classes
and half a loaf of a thesis short of an M.A.
did I, deep
in the middle of the night,
rise out of my Chairman's wife's bed
and, in my underwear,
crunch icy corn stalks under naked feet,
walk the fields behind their farmhouse
until dawn, coughing, shivering
and finally vomiting,
until I ended up in a squeaky hospital bed,
with pneumonia,
unable to stop weeping,
when out of the mist of my fever
a ghostly and boozy doctor appeared
to tell me to immediately leave
this incestuous place
and never return?

Why,
indeed.

5

Sometimes
at Swigge's desk, swiveling
inside the meticulously devised gloom
of Piranesi's dungeon,
I'm reminded of Ludwig's visual rooms
in which he perhaps also imagined
himself among arches, fleches and ropes
hanging out of the shadows
of such a prodigious formality . . .

"There is a lack of clarity about the role
of *imaginability* in our investigation,"
Ludwig said, wondering
perhaps where the staircases led,
what the vaults enclosed,
why the pulleys, ladders, catwalks,
gangways and chains couldn't disguise
an architecture as sublimely compromised
as the un-*imaginability* in Rossy's eyes
as his soul slowly expired,
while I, equally crucified,
stood there remembering
his dream of hair, blond auburn

red/black braided free hanging
windswept blue-tinged henna-streaked
sunlight-caressed
betrayed
and adored hair
rising
and falling follicles
of living light . . .

6

Already,
we'd been to two leather bars, a pool hall,
an Embarcadero tool and die shop,
so before the six trips with hand trucks
and dollies, hauling 100 boxes of candy,
cigarettes, syrup, dry-iced ice cream,
sandwiches, soups and nuts,
I was exhausted. Anything
dropped vanished
under the terrible surveillance
of five rows of pissed-off fluorescent-lit sailors,
waiting five rows deep behind a yellow line
for us (for me) to fill machines bolted
to the mess hall floor, each of us doing
exactly what Giggers did, zipping up
sharp edges without pause thumbs
corkscrewing and flipping amid catcalls:

"You on the rag, fella?"
"Your fat ass'd make good target practice
for the gooks, pal!"

The youngest and dumbest of us (not me!)
slipped in spilt orange syrup, cups flying
from splayed fingers like playing cards,
black and red goop brilliantly oscillated
before 500 astonished eyeballs,
Giggers whispering, "Forget it, keep goin'!"
until, swiping sweat, whistles pushed us
back away from a lunging tidal wave
of enraged punch-drunk centaurs,
breaking against quaking machines,
which, if a cup didn't fall immediately,
were assaulted by fists hips and groins,
mounted, it seemed, by a fury familiar
only to ancient gods, until,
appetites sated, bedlam receded
precipitously and we returned
to our metallic underlings, dazed, afraid,
and entirely unable to differentiate between
what the Chairman and Heidegger
understood to be the real and the true.

Everyone upstairs knew that Swigge,
who hid in a broom closet when
anyone visited, was also Mildred P. Willy
who initialed Home Relief requests
and Oscar Rappaport who signed off on
Old Age and Blind Assistance, each
answering the phone: "Raskolnikov speaking."
In three boxes in the L section, neatly labeled,
he kept his photography collection: girl on girl,
solos, B&D, artful and not-so-much-so,
in a toilet closet along with 35mm reels,
a rolled-up sheet and projector
and pharmaceutical supplies.

Everyone also knew he was obsessed
with one HHH, Harold Herman Hoeckstra,
an ingenious cheat who, under aliases,
received various kinds of assistance
and was being sought by every DSS department
in the state: "A Robin Hood with a Napoleonic
complex getting Blind Aid from Orange County
under W. Marcuse, M. McLuhan on
Supplemental Rent in Needles, leaves
thank-you notes, requests for LSD from Dr. T. Leary,
rants against 'mass and linear society'
by C. Guevara, the balls on this guy,
last year a drunken accordion-playing,
flamenco-dancing retired movie extra

named Paddy Edgecomb filed in Marin County
using the same ss number. And get this:
yesterday in the 3rd floor staff men's room
when a wad of tissue paper popped out
of a dispenser hole in the next stall
someone began quoting H.G. Wells on
the Mind being at the End of its Tether—
'with a frightful queerness come into life:
there is no way out or around or through;
it is the end.' Under the wall no shoes,
hands or hooves! I've seen him upstairs,
handing out pamphlets about electricity—
recruiting for some kind of revolution . . . ?"

Harold Herman Hoeckstra?
aka A.M. Ampère?
A urine-sprinkling visionary Robin Hood?
My pulse a good 40 knots,
hurricane on the horizon.

8

After the Kosmaczewskis murdered
Malka's husband and two sons,
wearing and eating proudly
the products of their labor,
Mother hid her Jewish neighbor,
Malka Piekarz, and her six-year-old daughter,

Gitele, in our woodshed, and when
the Kosmaczewskis informed on us
and the police took away our milk cows
and giant swine, Mashie, saying
next time they'd burn our barn down,
at school for the first time
I was called "Little Jew,"
everyone, my older brother, Leon,
and two sisters, Maria and Hela,
and my father, wandering the woods
at night, weeping, was frightened.
Everyone but Mother, who,
after our neighbors stopped suspecting us,
moved the Piekarzes out of the woods
and back into our house.

In Jedwabne, where for centuries
everyone worked and lived together,
everything about everyone was known,
except perhaps how profound the envy,
fear and hatred of and for the Jews.

Hide long enough from your fear,
Mother said,
and you too disappear.

Indeed,
here now, two stories deep,
surrounded by a ghostly tribe
of ever-prostrating,

ever-procuring souls of the despised,
I, beaten and shamed
into a nonentity,
a faceless surrogate,
a "Little Jew,"
despised enough to want to die,
can't help but envy them.

For a time the Zodiac despised
a phantom identity I shared,
seen by the US Army as mere fodder,
despised by Rossy's father,
yes, I too know hatred, and fear,
but never have I known the rapturous,
obstinate devoted hatred the Jews knew.

Who choose to continue to believe
they are loved by their God
beyond imaginability,
and thus remain Jews,
while I disown so much
of who and what I am.

Thus,
to my other sins
I must add the sin of envy.

9

After repairing, refilling, and surviving
the fifth and final naval assault,
Giggers took us up to the main deck,
where, light rinsing off rows
of neatly stacked aircraft,
the Golden Gate and the hills of the East Bay
gleaming beyond—all of it,
simply stupendous. Watching each
of his tobacco plumes dent the Pacific,
Giggers advised, "Don't judge those
who've been to hell
by what they do to machines."

Pavlov's theory of command,
desire, titillation,
and release playing out
in every direction,
infinitely . . .

Imagine a medieval tribe of tunnel-makers
warring against a civilization
so self-idealized as to believe
for their perpetuation such
magnificent killing machines
were a necessity.

Imagine Giggers, in praise,
reciting: "Displacement 60,000 tons,

length 1,047′ 6″, width 248′ 6″,
complement 4,000 men,
100 F-4B Phantom 11 aircraft,
CVA circa 1964 model just back from hell."

In other words,
founded in 1865 by Civil War veterans,
the Ku Klux Klan believed
"Whomever a man would naturally hate,
he hates a little more
because he has been a soldier."

10

"There is the fundamental paradox of the welfare
state: that it is not built for the desperate, but for
those who are already capable of helping themselves."

—MICHAEL HARRINGTON

Beginning one of his notebooks
with this quote Swigge goes on
to wonder how a Christian nation
can treat its poor so callously.
"Harrington never worked in a place like this,
a system where 'underbudgeting' is
designed to arbitrarily keep costs down
while acting as a defense against public attack.

The city and state thus appear magnanimous,
politicians fair-minded regulators of
the public good . . . until the closed cases
lead to starvation, child abuse and suicides
at rates so great they arouse the public's
conscience. Then it all starts again—
bigger budgets, closer supervision,
more MSW programs . . . while the poor
are blamed because according to our
Puritan tradition of self-reliance those
too weak or stupid to contribute get
pushed aside, deserve not to survive . . ."

II

A boy, on the shores of Lake Michigan,
I'd play dead, bury myself up
to my neck in sand,
sometimes hide under my covers,
imagining a hole in a hillside,
a cave under my living room floor,
or a hideout inside a tree
from which I'd observe the approach
of those looking for survivors.

Sometimes the isolation
was so unbearable I'd come out

only to be more afraid,
and alone, wishing
I'd never left my hiding place.

Ludwig said: "If a lion could talk,
we could not understand him . . .
What is internal is hidden from us . . ."

Once, after Rossy complained
about his father I asked him
to imagine a hole deep enough
for seven people to sleep, eat,
stretch, whisper, and defecate in.
To imagine the limits of such a place,
when to stand, stretch or speak
would require fierce examination.

Perhaps he refused to even try
because the language,
as Ludwig would say, involved
in perceiving such a landscape
and thought picture required
imagining someone else's hell.

12

Betty, who moved to San Francisco,
called me at work this morning.

Everyone, it appears, knows
exactly where I'm hiding.

We sat on a bench in Union Square Park,
under a transplanted eucalyptus tree,
her freckles accenting the intense sorrow
of her green eyes. The Chairman,
now also divorced from Aristotle,
sends his regards, she smiled.
After I left, he briefly considered misery
but instead chose Kierkegaard.
She too was complicit in a crime against me,
she said, choosing to love me over
feeling cast-off, which he'd counted on.
She'd come out here, I should understand,
not for me but for the time and place.

So there we sat, in the middle
of a park and a city and a millennium
obsessed with radical possibility,
devoid of even a hint of tranquillity
watching a hand puppet express hostility
at something another one said or thought.
"Everyone's coming here now," she said,
"because everywhere else seems
so empty and far behind."

Yes,
one could smell it everywhere,
the foul scent of complicity.

13

Yesterday,
in every San Francisco newspaper,
the Maniac thus spoke:

> "THIS IS THE ZODIAC SPEAKING. I AM THE MURDERER OF THE TAXI DRIVER OVER BY WASHINGTON ST & MAPLE ST LAST NIGHT, TO PROVE THIS HAVE IS A BLOOD STAINED PIECE OF HIS SHIRT. I AM THE SAME MAN WHO DID IN THE PEOPLE IN NORTH BAY AREA. THE S.F. POLICE COULD HAVE CAUGHT ME LAST NIGHT IF THEY HAD SEARCHED THE PARK PROPERLY INSTEAD OF HOLDING ROAD RACES WITH THEIR MOTORCYICLES SEEING WHO COULD MAKE THE MOST NOISE. THE CAB DRIVERS SHOULD HAVE JUST PARKED THEIR CARS & SAT THERE QUIETLY WAITING FOR ME TO COME OUT OF COVER. SCHOOL CHILDREN MAKE NICE TARGETS, I THINK I SHALL WIPE OUT A SCHOOL BUS SOME MORNING. JUST SHOOT OUT THE FRONT TIRE & THEN PICK OFF THE KIDDIES AS THEY COME BOUNCING OUT.⊕"

Naming his prey provoked satisfaction
for the Zodiac, deepening
the ecstasy of expectation
of further brutality. Thus
the invention of an ungrammatical logic
designed to hypnotize, hold hostage
and convince a multitude of ordinary citizens
to replace their reality with his own.
Quite ingenious, one could claim,
this replacing of everything

one once believed and loved
with a mythology (in his case astrology)
of such righteous self-celebration.

If,
as with Treblinka,
fate, perseverance,
and pure insane luck
permits a few to survive
then all the kiddies must be killed
because if even a few survive
the absolute fidelity and willful blindness
required in maintaining
such a mythology might collapse.

At times, in order to deaden
the ungrammatical logic of a reality
based on reimagining the past,
both mine and Mother's,
I've considered suicide. Believing
I'd survived enough already.

Believing, Ludwig said,
is not thinking. Sitting down
one must give no thought
to the possibility of a chair collapsing.

14

Swigge, in his notebooks,
explained Heddie's last name:
"Butterfly is her go-go dancer's moniker,
real name owns strained Irish/French/German
vowels warring unpronounceable Ukrainian
consonants, an escapee from an asylum
with six shock treatments, her shrink wrote:
'in constant flight.' Committed by her mother
after she tried to murder her with their
Easter ham, quite the looker, surreally blond,
long mountain-climbing legs and buns—yes,
hopeless blue/gray/green eyes, she catches
me staring and laughs, a fat four-eyed jerk
falling for a zonked out hippie hillbilly lioness . . .
God have mercy on these poor souls in
the R section seeing her posing . . . a stunning
wobbly-legged crane . . . they probably thought
they'd seen everything . . . I've arranged aid
for her in the name of three extinct clients,
plus all my pocket money—I'll probably end up
down here myself . . . and good riddance! . . ."

What should one make of this?
Sometimes sense hides in a hole
under a barn in eastern Poland.
Sometimes it's right before your eyes,
disguised as a wobbly-legged crane,
an unrecognizably ill-defined mistake

of stupendous proportions,
just waiting to materialize.

15

Mother wrote: "Our neighbors ordered
every Jew to dig a hole big enough
to bury other Jews, into which,
when completed, they were also put . . ."

An algorithm of infinite symmetry,
life serving death by expanding its bounty,
furthering its reach. Did the perpetrators
appreciate their satire? Yes, it was practical,
indignity as revenge, but for what?

Booklet 9 of Mother's diaries says:

. . . once on a German radio in the town square
we heard Hitler's voice, everyone German soldiers
our neighbors smiling at the crazy screaming,
a sound like fingernails on a blackboard trying
to scrape God's face from our minds . . . conquer
our souls as well as our bodies and minds . . .
Henryk looked so frightened—a wolf's howls
demanding we see the world the way it did . . .

. . . who will remember Jews lived next to us . . .
the sausages and cakes we brought to their funerals,
the dancing at weddings the good mornings
and good nights we bid each other the goods
we bought and sold . . . who will remember kindnesses
no matter how small or imagined . . .

at night sometimes I hear singing from our barn . . .
it can't be but . . . Polish at times, then Yiddish . . .
a woman's voice so piercing . . . so full of longing . . .
what does one long for when one has nothing . . .
one of God's angels come down to understand . . .

now only hatred and envy . . . yet God gave us the eyes
and hearts to know right from wrong . . . I'm so ashamed
I can't look in the mirror to comb my hair . . . what those
who look and dress and pray like me did . . .

when the Germans made them burn their holy books
I tried to imagine burning my grandma's bible from
which my mother read to me each night before bed . . .
they didn't also have grandmas and bibles . . . one day
Henryk will read this and remember . . . what we did
to other human beings like us . . .

so quickly it happened, hoodlums from other towns
came with blood already on their hands . . . to beat the sick
and dying, not Germans . . . but Poles . . . the head of a
thirteen year old girl tossed and kicked like a ball . . .
everyone bursting with joy . . .

when the Jews begged our priest to stop the massacre
that would disgrace every Pole forever he said every Jew,
young and old, was a communist, a traitor to Poland . . .
every member of his congregation hated Jews and not
one Christian leader would intervene . . . and he was right . . .
not one did . . .

So when Sleszynski offered his barn they all went house
to house, chasing the Jews into the streets, playing music . . .

16

Upstairs
four long and two short rings
means I must flee to—I believe—
the second-floor meeting room,
to escape from—yet again—sense
to nonsense, or at least pretend
to have somewhere to go.
But I prefer staying put and watching,
from one level below the primitive,
the endless conveyor belt of shaved,
scrubbed, stockinged appendages
flowing outside my window.
Each a complex system of muscles
and fibrous ligaments wrapped,
like colorful wires inside a switchboard,
around the most delicate bones
of the human carriage, connecting

idea to impulse, impulse to motion.
None though as bowed, small-boned,
as my own peasant legs, which
in their backward sway and inward turn,
shaped by years of adherence
to hostile terrains, possess
a history of staying put.

Basically, tell someone
you're a clerk and they squint, blink,
cough and sometimes spit
because the word calls to mind
someone in sleeve garters
and a green eyeshade,
performing perfunctory acts
that signify a sanctioned,
frenzied, colorless legitimacy.
Calls to mind someone
who prefers to be left alone.

I prefer to be left alone.

FOUR

Henryk Stanislaw Wyrzykowski Stops

In the Squalor of the Waiting Room,

Begrudgingly

After the Zodiac fulfilled his prophecy,
the real reason Ruby let me drive again, he said,
wasn't because nobody else would,
but because he liked the fact
that I didn't seem to mind
being called shithead. "So far, shithead,
you've made us exactly nothing.
Improve on that today."
Mostly old ladies returning from an IGA,
drunks enraged by last calls,
cast-out husbands taken to hotels,
sailors seeking Tenderloin bliss,
and a seriously stoned orthodontist
looking for a misplaced convention.

Then,
just before quitting time,
Ruby sent me to a Fillmore alley,
where a bearded black man inflated
in black leather, asked me to please
pop the trunk, into which he dropped
a large canvas-covered bundle.
Climbing in the front seat, noticing me
notice what looked like a revolver butt
jutting out of his left ventricle,
he smiled and said, "Hey—I'm Hatch,
because that's what people say

I'm always doing, hatching things.
We got a few more stops.
Just be cool now, Tonto, okay!"

2

I did two things this morning
I promised myself never to: pause
while passing through the waiting room.
Pause anywhere in these corridors
and you get spat at slapped
buttonholed and otherwise requisitioned,
but stop in this maze of fluorescent-lit
sepia-sprayed beseeches to read a sign:
WHAT YOU SHOULD KNOW
IF YOU HAVE AN EMERGENCY;
QUESTIONS AND ANSWERS
and someone will step up
and holler in your face: "Hey—
I'm an EMERGENCY—a shit-stinking
jobless Superglue-addicted
trash-eating cardboard-living lowlife!
Know what Margaret Mead said
a healthy personality was?
The opposite of me . . .
QUESTIONS AND ANSWERS?! . . .
like why didn't I finish fourth grade,
get arrested eighteen times before I was sixteen

take it up the ass when I like pussy—hey!—
we're all thieves pimps and mama's boys . . .
give a guy a buck, Roosevelt,
and like a nightmare I disappear . . ."

Buck in hand, he vanished before
I could wipe his spit off my face,
before my memory of A.M. Ampère
sprinkling piss and wearing a soiled sheet
could coalesce—ah! Swigge's bogeyman
HHH—Harold Herman Hoeckstra
aka H. Ford and T. Edison?

A treatise on an Emergency,
a Margaret Mead mockery,
a Superglue-addicted specter, alive
in the spicy mélange of the waiting room?
His raison d'être not Robin Hood,
but a Christ wannabe crucifying himself
in order to deny his tormentors the pleasure . . .

3

In a dream I'm holding Rossy
down in a field while a rabbi
dressed like a policeman
attempts to un-circumcise him
because he converted to Catholicism.

Looking up at me, he asks if
it was I who informed on him.
I lie and say no, it was his father.

I awake holding his head
which I remember was cut off
and kicked around our front yard
like a soccer ball during the
Jedwabne pogrom. The Survivor
is yelling at me to put it back
where it belongs on the shelf
in his garage with all the others.
Only a Nazi, he screams, wouldn't know
where things belong,
would so wholeheartedly
destroy one's dignity.

Yes, I think,
only half dreaming,
once a Nazi always a Nazi.

4

It's June 6th 1968 and today
Robert Kennedy is laid to rest
beside his murdered brothers
John F. and M.L. King,
and now we're all spent,

uninspired, less talented,
and more obscene. Today
even the pigeons appear unwilling
to open their leaden wings,
the solemn sky is staring at the earth,
which seems only too willing
to accept more grief.

Usually
our frankfurter lunches
in Union Square Park are a treat,
but today Betty isn't looking at me,
saying, "I came out here thinking
maybe being so far away would
make me feel less inconsequential,
but I was wrong. Evil doesn't keep score."

Today
the world is more treacherous,
and no longer represented
by actual or possible thought,
which Ludwig said makes up
the whole of reality.

5

Eureka!
It's closing time, the end

of the 73rd Monday
of my basement tenure,
and around me everything is floating,
a symphony of hissing, clanging radiators
and engorged pipes, the main floor
and streets, my very desk, where
I listen to psychedelic prophecies
on my transistor radio, sleep, write
and read sad esoteric testimonies
in this antiquated filing system
which Swigge claimed he organized
"according to Tacitus' rhetorical, moral
and ethnographic use of history,
as outlined in his *Germania*"
(which, he noted: compared Roman
decadence to barbarian vitality),
"because nothing can be found down here . . ."
—all floating toward closing time,
known here as a state of mind,
a belief in collaborations,
a sphere of ever-waning influence,
an anthropological phenomenon
in which my colleagues soon
will be hurrying toward bars, movies,
illicit liaisons, walk for miles, revisit
youthful memories in an attempt
to escape the holistic view of themselves
as members of a sad beleaguered experiment
at diligence and empathy
once again coming to a close.

6

Even before we crossed the Bay Bridge
and I was told to stop behind a shaky warehouse
on the Oakland docks where another
bundle-carrying leather-encased black man
performed inscrutable acts of transfer
I was petrified. Drugs, guns, counterfeit loot—
whatever, I was complicit. Hatch,
his hand light on my shoulder, anticipating
our ipso facto transactions, chuckled:
"Think of this as a new beginning!
We're Bonnie and Clyde no, Romulus
and Remus, founding a new nation,
reinventing the wheel!"

Now he and the second man,
Dingy, his jacket wide open, exposing
a holstered revolver, began,
as we moved down and around back roads,
humming
and slapping knees, seats,
and me, to the tune of "Sugar in the Morning . . ."
enjoying themselves enormously.
Then, crossing the bridge back
to San Francisco, Hatch said, "Sometimes
it's beautiful, sometimes it aint,
we drop in and out, live a hundred years,
maybe a minute, but what it is, my man,
is all at once: 'nam Buddhist anarchist antichrists—
If you gotta blame something,

blame the gods Envy and Greed
whom everyone worships,
blame our man Camus who described
the absurd as a dude armed with a sword
attacking machine guns . . ."

Then, giving me a big squeeze,
he said, "One more stop and
your night's work is done.
Just be cool, man, be cool!"

7

The night before we went
to the railroad tracks Rossy told me
what the Survivor told him:
They replaced his name with a number,
took his clothes shoes and hygiene,
made him crawl like a snake,
but deep inside his soul was unscathed.
His mother father two sisters one brother
and thirteen uncles and aunts they took,
but not his faith. At night he prayed to die
but never once did he hate his life.
His mind and flesh they took
but what most they wanted,
his will to live, that he hid.

But I found it.
Killing his son, I did
what even the Nazis couldn't.

8

Though I treat my memories
concerning Mother cordially,
somehow they seem to know
I resent them, and act as if
they don't really care. Haughty,
domineering, and full of spleen,
they mix fantasy with hearsay,
add pieces of my dreams
and diced feelings to form
a reality mostly devoid of me.
At age two I went to our barn
with Mother to feed our Jews.
A memory insists it can still smell
their filthy clothes, the rot between
their toes that they tried to wash off
in the pig trough every other Tuesday.
That I can see five adults, a teenage boy
and a girl no older than me, lying
side by side in a hole as deep
as a barn door, as wide as our horse stall,
insists it can see, in the dawn's light,
their eyes, startled out of sleep,

gazing up into mine, then quickly
looking away, as if to spare me
the shame of their wretchedness.
They understood it insists
why I withdrew my hand
as they reached for cups of milk,
porridge, slices of black bread,
never imagining how much I craved
a portion of Mother's love for them.

Can I really smell the shit pot I emptied,
hear Mother's screaming
for me to run into the woods
as fists broke her cheekbones,

because even they knew
she wouldn't say where
our Jews were hidden?

9

This time we stop under the Embarcadero,
where a third black man in a black van
with painted windows, reverses the transfer,
loading, with Dingy's help, the bundles
into the van, while Ruby screams,
"WHERE YOU NOW—FUCKIN RENO!!??"
until Hatch turns my radio off.

"The trick is not to give a shit. Know why
white slave owners gave their black babies
their mothers' names? So they'd stay property!"

Meanwhile, Higgs, the new guy,
is threatening to kick Dingy's ass
all the way to San Jose if he doesn't stop
telling him to hurry up! while Hatch,
sighing, says, "Everything except death
is status quo . . . remember who told you that . . ."

Their work done, Hatch, Dingy and I
are following Higgs and the van back
into the Fillmore district, to another alley,
where I'm told to stop. "Try to imagine
how happy you're making people
with all this stereo equipment . . ."
In the rearview mirror I'm nodding,
eyes sickly gray. "Anybody asks—say
we're the National Guard Auxiliary
and these are ballots for the next election."
This as Dingy leans over and cuts
my mike cord with a switchblade.
"It's okay, be scared, my man,
be glad you're scared,
I got the gun and I'm scared!"

After paying me the meter plus
a ten-spot, they're gone
and now Ruby is screaming

because once again nobody
is answering him.

10

In his notebooks Swigge continues:
"No one hates the poor more than the poor,
who beat, steal and kill each other daily,
sit in our waiting room waiting to die.
Mrs. Patrick, a black woman with
four children, lived on semimonthly
AFDC payments of $105.70. Due to illness
her oldest child missed school so
her worker, visiting without notice,
smelled whisky on her breath, concluding
she was neglecting her children.
She worked two part-time jobs but
couldn't afford a car or feed her kids
without our help. Few civilized societies
would blame her for her situation.
Raised in a single-family home, one
of four kids, a teenage mother high school
dropout—she didn't exactly deal herself
this hand, sit down one morning and plan
this life for herself. Know what we did?
We said in order to continue getting aid
two of her children would be placed in
foster homes. Yes, either she gives up

two or loses sustenance for all. When
she refused, her case was closed . . . if
a client doesn't appear grateful or compliant
cases are closed, applying a second,
third time makes them obedient . . . master
and slave. A storyline going all the way back
to Egypt . . . today it's called 'overbudgeting' . . .

"Diogenes, believing poverty a virtue,
lived in a tub in the center of Athens,
begging being superior to enslaving others . . .
what would he make of our Philosophy:
'to provide financial, medical & social services
to all eligible people,' to respect 'the right
of every individual to achieve and maintain
personal dignity and full self-determination' . . . ?"

Probably,
he wouldn't be down here with me,
hiding behind a desk,
but out there in the middle of things,
deep in the waiting room,
sitting in a tub full of tears . . .

II

A basement is a place beneath
something else, a place lower down,

deeper and darker than what's above.
A world defined by what it's under.

Rossy existed in a world
beneath mine, a place impacted
with facts and figures, the language
of irretrievable guilt.

His mother, also a survivor,
seldom left her bed. Once he asked
what being loved felt like.
Embarrassed, we both laughed.
Mother made room in her faith for me.
Not being made room for isn't something
a seventeen-year-old boy can contemplate.
Imagine asking such a question.

Hiding is existing
in a constant state of alarm,
remaining undiscovered, and inferior.

Maybe
he placed the soup can on his head
so casually and compliantly
because beneath everything else
he knew he'd already
suffered enough.

The hair colorful plumage growing
out of faces, shoulders, arms and legs
all moving down Haight Street
miles in both directions,
or so it seems anyway,
everything fecund, growing out
of everything else, a parade,
Betty called it, having lured me
outside again, everyone screaming,
"Down with LBJ's War Machine,"
pleased with themselves, dancing up
Haight to the Fillmore and down
to the Panhandle, ending on Hippie Hill
for a Being-In in Golden Gate Park,
call it sweet pandemonium, signs
advertising glories of indigence,
"Today's the first day of the rest of your Life,"
girls serenading soldiers lined up
on either side of the street, boys
attempting seriousness behind
stern faces, eying un-holstered breasts,
police phalanxes blocking side streets,
National Guard jeeps fitted with
machine guns, reminding us
this is a nation of laws, of wrath
and vengeance, of Roman fire and spirit,
"They're all here today," Betty screams,
"pray some idiot doesn't start shooting!"

Indeed,
we're in pursuit of knowledge,
and happiness, a carnival on the cusp
of a funeral, a magnificent medley
of vanities, a dung heap of souring
good intentions, a Florence imbued
with malevolence, Eros sprawled
and ripening over Betty's freckled face
on my lap, a taxonomic stick being passed
back and forth, its cloud big as Byzantium.
"The world's high enough," I giggled,
"No, not nearly," says she, watching
belly dancers clipping castanets, girls
somersaulting an agile, breezy Sanskrit,
youth celebrating itself with banjos
guitars sopranos serenading early stars,
this grassy shining, transplanted sky,
boasting of exotic lineage, "The future
will hate our recklessness, not a true believer
in the crowd, don't you love it!"

Yes,
an apostle army of Einsteins, Calibans
and Maharishi Mahesh Yogis—swashbucklers
all turning orthodoxy on its head . . .
never a time like this . . .
and never again . . .

13

A new letter from the Zodiac
in the morning newspaper:

> "I LIKE KILLING PEOPLE BECAUSE IT IS SO MUCH FUN IT IS MORE FUN THAN KILLING WILD GAME IN THE FORREST BECAUSE MAN IS THE MOST DANGEROUE ANAMAL OF ALL TO KILL SOMETHING GIVES ME THE MOST THRILLING EXPERIENCE IT IS EVEN BETTER THAN GETTING YOUR ROCKS OFF WITH A GIRL THE BEST PART OF IT IS THAE WHEN I DIE I WILL BE REBORN IN PARADICE AND THEI HAVE KILLED WILL BECOME MY SLAVES I WILL NOT GIVE YOU MY NAME BECAUSE YOU WILL TRY TO SLOI DOWN OR ATOP MY COLLECTIOG OF SLAVES FOR MY AFTERLIFE EBEORIETEMETHHPITI "

If it's true, as Ludwig believed,
that the meaning of words
signify their function
in every language game,
what then is the function here?

A belief in reincarnation,
faith in a paradise? Slavery
in an afterlife, certainly.
One must remember,
his too is a human mind.

Hitler exterminated the patients
of mental hospitals, children and the sick,
the poor and weak, and those

he considered sexually and socially deviant,
and therefore unproductive.
Without a doubt, if possible,
he would've killed Ludwig,
with whom, in Linz, he attended
the *Realschule*, though he,
a bourgeoisie wannabe,
wouldn't have associated
with an ex-Jewish aristocrat
with an appetite for suicide,
high culture, homosexuality
and a mind munificent enough
to imagine a world of language and reality.

No, reality isn't what Hitler wanted,
or expected. Though, given time,
like the Zodiac, he might've conquered
and colonized paradise.

14

Now Heddie,
a once-every-other-week habit,
appears out of the shadows
to lay down with me in the Z section,
among the Zelmers, Zeemans and Zyluks—
Zyluk being a name I especially like
because Jozef Zyluk was a Jedwabne boy

I played with before he,
along with his father and ten uncles,
decided murder was the answer
to all their problems.

Unlit by fluorescence
or the window light reflected in mirrors
Swigge installed at the far dead end
of a cul-de-sac of long-forgotten echoes,
the spot where he kept blankets,
magazines, condoms and candles
locked in a box Heddie led me to
as if following a trail of breadcrumbs.

Looking forward to her next visit
even before her present one
happened, I'd roam the aisles,
jealous of imaginary faces ogling
her go-go dancing, the girls she posed with
in Swigge's photos, of, insanely,
the identical quarter-moon beauty marks
on each flat buttock, or the way
in which the inclines of her hips
outlined her cowhide miniskirt,
even that sometimes she called me Swigge,
or without explanation would and
wouldn't appear. Therefore,
sometimes after work not wanting
to return to my two tiny rooms
in the Mission District, I'd go

to a ramshackle all-night art deco movie palace
on Market Street and sit high
in the wobbly balcony darkness,
listening to un-ecstatic gunshots
and noir screams to appease
my own echoing pleas
for forgiveness.

Perhaps
this is why I decided,
for a reason unknown to me,
to ask Heddie to move in with me?

And why
she looked so stricken
and changed the subject?

15

After booklet 9 of Mother's diaries,
the language begins to break up,
splintering the syllables to half-tones,
shards of ideas fleeing their subtext,
images conjuring their opposites,
meaning surrendering its logic,
all of which I'm trying to fix.
The later sections are becoming
nearly impossible to translate,
what Ludwig meant by ". . . to bring light

into one brain or another—but,
of course, it is not likely."
I'm suffering doubtful feelings,
trying to fill in missing logic,
without forgoing any attempt at literality . . .

Booklet 10 begins in medias res
as they all to some extent do:

. . . zydokomuna they were called . . . communist Jews
we could hate better maybe, like everyone didn't
kiss up to the Russians . . . more a matter of not wanting
to share our martyrdom . . . as if Christ doesn't know
who lives where, whose work earned which house
boots coats . . . belonged to . . . kill a child and your soul
turns black as the ash you turn them into . . .

when they the young couple came to my door
from hiding in the woods . . . I thought of my family,
my life means something . . . but their eyes
so frightened . . . it's getting harder to remember . . .
human beings, young and in love . . . should I also
only have eyes for their clothes, her mother's
wedding ring . . . charge them money and throw
them out when it's gone . . . my neighbors, if they
find out, will think I'm getting rich and come
looking for their share . . . good Christians . . .

then others heard and came seeking refuge also . . .

so we dug a hole in our barn big enough for four
to stand while three sleep . . . breathing I still hear
from my bedroom above the kitchen . . . fearing
my neighbors could also . . . mostly the wind
which doesn't care if someone's a Jew . . . none
of the animals in the barn do, cows chickens
hate nothing . . . feel no shame at who they are . . .
one day someone will read this know one family
loved God and all His creatures . . . it's so lonely
for the children . . . once we had twenty-eight cousins,
sixteen uncles and aunts, two grandpas one grandma . . .
no one visits now . . . but compared to our Jews . . .
no rabbi Ibram . . . the butcher Jaakov Turberg
and his wife Ester, Morris the kheyder teacher
Mr. Danowska, father of Morris' best friend,
Mr. Itzhak Adamski . . . Malka and her children
we found hiding in the woods, the heads of
Malka's husband, Itzhak, their oldest girl,
Rywka, bashed in running outside our house . . .
clubs, shovels, pitchforks kitchen knives . . .
the Piekarzes too scared not to come with us . . .
everyone shouting it's time to settle things
with those who crucified Jesus Christ, take
Christian blood for matzoh . . . the source of all evil . . .

then on Sunday July 6th, not one German present,
the murderers came from Wasosz to Radzilow
having killed all the Jews there . . . hiding in the forests
Jews were told it was safe to return . . . then killed
and buried alive in a pit . . . no one lifting a finger . . .

hundreds of years suddenly not one Jew in Radzilow . . .
the survivors coming here . . .

to Jedwabne . . . to my back door . . .

16

In Swigge's notebook, he pasted this:

Home Relief Cases Closed March 1968 due to:
      Refusal to accept employment,
      Comply with departmental requirements
      Moved to other county
      Whereabouts Unknown
Decreases in resources due to:
      Illness, injury, discharge, death, exhaustion
      Reduction of U.I.B. or other income
      Departure of parent because of divorce or other person
      Discontinued support from non-legally responsible person
      Father outside home, other person outside home . . .
Our Monthly Statistical Report, January 1968, vol. 29 no. 1
Aid to Dependent Children:
      The number of applications received increased
      from 5,705 in December to 7,445 in January, or by 1,740.
      Cases added increased by 428, from 4,875 to 5,303,
      while cases closed increased by 753, from 2,423 to 3,176.
      The excess of cases added over closed was 2,127 in January,
      as compared with 2,452 in December.

The average grant per case increased by $4.02, from
$250.81 to $254.83.
Total grants in January were $35,307,589.

Swigge commenting: "Ask about these numbers
and you hear other numbers. As usual,
the fate of the poor hangs upon the decision
of those concerned only with what those
above them think. An endless cycle of egotism,
self-sympathy. You see it everywhere here,
those too weak and ashamed to defend themselves
are blamed for their own misfortune.
Separated and debased, they're swept deeper
under society's carpet, thus the richest society
in the history of the world lacks the will and
conscience to end poverty while the poor
become the victims of their own spiritual
and physical misery . . ."

In other words,
according to Swigge,
our job is to hide from the public's view
the suffering and helplessness
of the constituents of our largest minority,
and thereby further diminish them
in their eyes and in ours.

FIVE

Henryk, in Trying to Earn a Living Teaching

Spelling as a Second Language,

Learns a Thing or Two Himself,

About

the Quid Pro Quo of Death

1

Having smuggled something mysterious
back and forth between the East Bay
and San Francisco my hands shook
every time I tried to climb into a cab
so once again I ended up in line
waiting for food stamps, for sustenance,
until I found part-time work
teaching Spelling 1 and Arithmetic 2
to rich South Koreans and Saudi Arabians,
at Harold's Business School on Market Street,
speaking v-e-r-y s-l-o-w-l-y
for a little over minimum wage,
wearing a new old Salvation Army tie
and bruised, asymmetrical jacket,
a haircut provided by a cross-eyed
ex-piano teacher I met in line,
chin and cheeks shaven
while my split upper lip kept
its hairy camouflage—but hey
suddenly I was igniting a blackboard
with rules about what does and doesn't happen
when *i* goes before *e* and 18 is extracted
from 26 before being savaged by 3
after 6 is forsaken, which was why
I was up half the night reading
basic manuals until the morning
of the day I was asked to teach Speech 1

and maybe 2 to soldiers irregularly
stationed at the Presidio.
Thirty-five young glazed eyes
staring at the floor or ceiling
and very far out the windows,
at anything but where the skinny weirdo
was struggling to explain a few simple principles
about human discourse to those
seriously suffering from a variety
of mostly severe nervous disorders
after enduring twenty-two straight months
of utter hell.

2

Waiting in line here takes discipline,
a state of mind similar
perhaps
to Zarathustra's "grunting swine"
whose scrupulous denunciations
are born of wounded vanity
and an undying self-contempt.
Waiting in line means sleeping standing up,
disappearing into the wilderness
of one's molecular constitution,
playing deaf and dumb,
not stepping on anyone else's bunions,
though most of all keeping one's pulse

well below 22–23 knots,
a very strong breeze,
and thus not suffering a bad case
of the dreads out loud,
means moving every forty minutes
maybe three inches,
having one's shirtfront coated with,
say, gouts of blood, spit and rotgut,
enduring
the stink of sweat, urine, cheap cologne,
being elbowed, pushed and shoved,
while never once taking personally
anything anyone says or does
before, behind, between and among,
especially the signs over barred windows,
or even one's own sour breath,
bouts of acid reflux, bad karma,
memories of freezing rain,
existential hallucinations,
means someone tattooed with blistering profiles
of Jesus H. Christ on each enraged bicep
turning to ask whether,
ultimately
you consider yourself a victim
of your own stupidity,
or not.

3

The morning before I killed his son
the Survivor explained to Rossy
exactly what a Sonderkommando did:
disposed of bodies filled suitcases
and freight cars with the things
only the living needed: nail clippers hats
nylons boots pillows umbrellas
pencils pots eyeglasses tools
mirrors and precious metals
with and without pieces of gums attached—
everything owned, worked for,
cooked with, used to look and feel good in,
like: smelling salts nose hair clippers
baby rattlers toys photos of wives
and boyfriends diaries buttons prayer books
histories of the Middle Ages salves
for nosebleeds address and date books—
things to be sold to pay for more death . . .
but he dreamed only of women's hair
freight cars full of blond steel gray black
raisin still-braided beautiful women's hair . . .

Standing
not a hundred feet away
in a railroad dump outside of Chicago,
balancing a soup can on his head,
Rossy seemed to be
for a moment at least,

looking up at me
from a frozen hole in the earth,
one of *those* Jews,
eyes pleading
for a little more of something . . .

4

After an Allen Ginsberg reading
at the I & Thou Cafe on Haight Street,
owned by a Martin Buber–loving
ex-Hasid lowroller from Brooklyn,
Ginsberg chanting, "Hmmmmmm O
Satyananda say OM Kali Pada Guha Roy
whose yoga gives ecstasy!"
we walked up rowdy Haight amid
the various tribes of pranksters
and radical provocateurs, Betty sighing,
"You need to get out more, buddy"
passing head shops, record stores,
posters of Malcolm X, Ho-Ho-Ho-Chi Minh
Einstein sticking out an unending tongue,
competing lifestyles "Farm for Jesus"
and "Better Living Through Chemistry,"
doorways playing banjos, harmonicas
and electric harpsichords, stoop-sitters
incanting lurid lullabies, SNCC & Young Socialists
reps protesting one another, for and against

symbolic lobotomy and sober amnesia,
CBS interviewing a vegetarian bakery . . .
A moment devoid, it seemed, of a tragic sense,
exhilaration as elixir, Faust welcoming
a world "governed by demons," the forces
of reaction pushed to the brink
of a beautiful recklessness, everywhere
a wretched pandemonium, Buber's exulting
"the hallowing of the everyday."

All of which
only makes me miss
my dungeon paradise.

5

Swigge,
in an attempt to enlarge
his perspective on this forlorn building,
and understand the underlying patterns
of a social phenomenon in which
human activity interrelates with
the behavior of other species,
such as lice, fungi, cats, dogs, pigeons
and an occasional snake,
in a desperate struggle to adapt
to often violent, unalterable social patterns,
read Claude Lévi-Strauss. Because,

for the most part, in these halls
instinct doesn't exist: "it's a kind
of Konrad Lorenz study in ethnology,
natural selection turned inside out,
sex not for mating but distraction,
Aristotle's pyramid in reverse with
the simplest creatures at top,
stripped of human characteristics,
a pecking order in which despair
fights paranoia to be first in line,
why with one eye open so many sleep,
curled incurably, giant infants on sofas
sucking thumbs, staring at walls,
an uninhabitable habitat no one adapts to,
evolves out of, the camel's neck evolving
backwards, reaching nothing, an ecosystem
in which only the most savage prevail . . .
in Nature's great scheme so insignificant
it's already forgotten . . ."

6

Thirty-five mostly empty eyes,
one hidden under an eye patch,
staring at wherever I
and the blackboard aren't,
as somewhere below sea level
I diagram a simple English sentence:

"The way to hell leads through the trees"
revised by me from the manual
("The way to the well . . .") in order
to skip over logical fallacies
(chapter 2) and thus ignore
the somatic powers of semiconsciousness
upon spaced-out oddly inflamed eyeballs,
I ask a few questions: Is death a subject
or an object, what idea, cause or belief
is worth killing one's fellow human beings for,
is sacrificing one's precious life
worth post-traumatic disorder,
the way through hell, paralysis,
being naïve and vulnerable the price
one needs to pay? Spaced-out, asleep—
without fear I can say anything!
It's misleading, Ludwig said, to call words
a description of a mental state,
instead we must call them "a signal."
The signal in their eyes?
That they no longer actually exist?
Boys mostly, in search of a subject,
all action once, but no longer.
Head in arms, a blond boy near the door
moans in his sleep, shirt soaked through,
eyes twitching, his dream a filter
through which boredom, constant fear
and fatigue flow, a blueprint of despair,
kicked suddenly awake by the boy
beside him, "C'mon, man, sit up!

You know what happens if we don't play along!"
Pupils dilated, dry lips smacking, biding his time
till the bell rings, they're pretending
to want a high school diploma, believe
in a future, don't know or care that now
that they can't fight they're useless.
At the bell the blond boy lifts himself
to march with the others, a slow orderly
procession of bewildered, nondescript
and sapped homo sapiens returning from
the Trojan Wars, Gettysburg and Dunkirk,
following the road through the endless trees
that leads to hell.

7

When Rossy was nine the Survivor explained,
drawing diagrams, how Treblinka
was actually two camps, I and II,
one for machinery and one for murder,
surrounded by a perimeter
of barbed wire fences,
the branches-covered inner one
concealing six gas chambers,
a crematorium, gallows, and large pits
filled mostly with Jews. To disguise it
as a transit camp new arrivals
were greeted with a Hebrew inscription

over the main entrance: "This is a gate
through which the righteous pass,"
a Star of David over each gas chamber,
which is why they were told
to write postcards encouraging
relatives and friends to move east
for "resettlement."

A better name for Jews
was the Selected People, he said,
because selection was both
their hope and punishment.
To the left the strong were selected,
to the right women, children,
the weak and sick, shaven and undressed,
waited inside "showers" to be suffocated,
their despoiled, shriveled bodies
searched for valuables by the husbands,
fathers and brothers of previous victims,
then buried only to be excavated
and incinerated, and buried again,
only to be dug up
and searched one final time.

Imagine,
the Survivor asked:
245,000 Warsaw Jews
112,000 from around Warsaw
735,000 residents of the General Government
7,000 from Slovakia

8,000 from Theresienstadt
4,000 from Greece
7,000 from Macedonia—

750,000 souls starved,
beaten, hanged
and worked to death,
then gassed and incinerated,
their souls never once deemed valuable
enough to be laid to rest.

8

Before
Mother's mind became inundated
with protein and silence,
she sometimes wondered
whether, after all the rage,
her neighbors' mirrors
returned the same faces,
stares and eyes
and exuberant personalities.
Greed she understood,
but such shamelessness . . .

All devils, she said,
speak the same language.

9

As the manual insisted,
on week 2 the pros and cons
of splitting infinitives must be discussed,
mentioning that to some grammarians
it was acceptable, others not.
To juice things up I quoted
the opening line from *Star Trek*:
to boldly go where no man has gone before . . .
Usually we get along, I fake enthusiasm
and they interest. With twenty-eight
minutes to go, and no one asleep, I,
the object of polite indifference,
needing to kill time, asked a bullish man
in the front row what he thought
of grammatical rules like this.
His half-shut eyes enjoying a drugged stupor,
he slowly lifted his head, grunting
"What de fuck?" Everyone awake now,
I backed into the blackboard, stuttering:
"Well, whaddya think, split the fuckers?"
Amid strained laughter, a soldier near me
said, "Don't ask him that, or anything!"
Unable to find my tongue, I shut my mind
as the man slowly rose toward an enormity
I'd never seen before. Finally,
an apology (for what?) squeaked out.
Then, cheeks inflamed by blood, he shook
the tremendous flatiron of his forehead,

his eyes staring past me to the blackboard.
Eclipsed, nobody looked at anyone else.
An endless moment lurching toward solemnity . . .
Off every wall his voice echoed: "You ever kill a man?"
My head tried to nod, but my mind wouldn't budge.
"That's yes or no? Tell me, I want to know!"
"Yes, once, a long time ago."
"Not much fun, eh?" I started crying.
Slow easy sputtering rising into raw sobbing.
Surprised, he walked over and wrapped me
in his arms. "Okay, man, I know, we're all
just poor sick animals, it's in our nature,
not really our fault . . ."

Everyone rose simultaneously
with the bells and walked out,
leaving us there, sobbing.
Stepping back to look at me, he said,
"I killed thirty-two men, boys some . . .
you'll never know what I've seen . . ."
and, walking away, paused at the door
to add, "It's a solecism, but you know that."

Yes,
I knew that.

10

Swigge,
not long before his death, wrote:
"Last week a new outbreak in Marin County
of A. Lincolns applying for Emergency Services,
specifying Adult Protection, given to persons
18 or older, physically or mentally disabled.
Apparently, the name didn't alarm the worker,
though Abe's answer to the mental health
survey gave pause: Have you ever received
mental health treatment? Attempted suicide?
Taken psychiatric drugs?—*All of the Above,*
he answered. A satirist, like Euripides,
playing us with his version of a satyr play,
half/man half/goat urine wit sprinkling
in the waiting room . . . now Lou Phillips telling
the hoity polloi upstairs we gotta stop Hoeckstra
before the press gets wind trying to increase
his own budget . . . says I'm trading sex for aid . . .
true, but so is he and with the same girl!
Mrs. Cafiso saw Heddie going into his office
twice last week, our blind elevator driver
Rev. Bingo overheard him offering her
increased heating/utility aid . . . sticking it
to us both . . . Marxists love chaos, about me
he's telling everyone . . . she broke our two last dates . . .
Two goat men fighting over a headcase . . .
Homo habilis, one step down from Erectus,
everywhere in these halls, no one escapes

his nature, Euripides thought laughter
the best weapon . . . still maybe I should get rid
of my films and photos . . . ?"

II

Rossy's crush on Gloria Talbot,
the B-movie Scream Queen
meant nothing to me then
but now his posters of *The Cyclops,*
Daughter of Dr. Jekyll and *The Leech Woman*
that covered his bedroom walls
visit my dreams. The Survivor's calling her
a "cheap shiksa tramp" only increased
his passion for analyzing every movie,
memorizing her every line of dialogue,
mooning over her TV Pocahontas,
goddess of the trees and rivers,
rising up in cowhide to instruct his dreams
on the sexual wealth of his nature.

Rossy,
who couldn't knot a tie,
get his hair to stay down, in love
with the Queen of the American Wilderness,
suddenly more than a clumsy,
bespectacled, inward protégé of atrocity,
someone excited about the future,

going off to college, leaving Chicago,
and his father.

Afterwards,
I found in his wallet a glamour photo
stamp-signed: "Thanks for writing,
fans like you make all the difference!
Hugs and kisses, Gloria."

Pocahontas,
a story without Jews,
and Treblinka.

12

It's true,
Betty makes me get out more . . .
away from Mother's diaries . . . someone
she knew at the Fillmore let us in
a back door to see the Beatles
debut their new White Album,
so now we're scrunched inside
an auditorium, ceiling craters spilling
pulsating color over floors and walls,
aching with celestial distress, oyster
shells leapfrogging terrorized chickens,
eggs re-hatching themselves,
a Daffy Duck DJ sounding the charge,

shadows clamoring Jimi Hendrix,
Carlos Santana and the Allman Brothers,
a Milky Way-stenciled ceiling
moving sideways, eyes closed,
Betty's dancing with herself,
the dance floor throbbing, aglitter
with beads and lace, swinging girls
high-kicking their grandmas' high-buttons,
all inside a gigantic fish tank, trays of
party favors floating past, neither of us
indulging, everyone else inside nirvana's
joyous bauble of bouncing satisfaction,
as lights dim over Bill Graham introducing
John Lennon's solemn image all the way
from London bedazzling a screen
over the stage, introducing "Revolution 1,"
"Blackbird," "Helter Skelter," "Sexy Sadie,"
"Happiness Is a Warm Gun" . . . his sonorous
sorrow a rhapsody crisscrossing
the Atlantic on high and low notes,
a spiraling expectation designed
to replace the merely magical
with a splendid and sanctified moment
of youth.

13

Because a cop shot back,
the Zodiac decided not just to kill
one back but make everyone wear
an astrological sign of his or her choosing,
and maybe blow up a school bus
or police station. Domination by threat,
blackmail, and conjecture. The paranoid's
reversal of social evolution back
to the Hominidae. Similar, one could say,
to our neighbors' behavior,
first threatening, then hiding,
then blackmailing Jews.
But the Zodiac worked for a living,
a man of his word (*the* word, in fact),
he owned a car, a house maybe,
paid his phone bill, entertained scruples,
made distinctions. He wasn't after money,
didn't cut off tongues, pluck out eyes,
burning to death hundreds at one time
never occurred to him, I don't think.
He preferred the intimacy
of face-to-face eradication.

Our neighbors were country folk
of simple stock, who couldn't say no
to a gold mine in their backyard,
wealth without labor. Theft,
maybe torture and murder,

didn't bring dishonor as long
as everyone did it, and nearly
everyone did, centuries of envy
and resentment gone with a little fire.
Social scientists tell us the norm
is what everyone accepts.
The norm isn't anyone's fault.

A quiet passionate storm
spreading farm to town. Not glory
or a desire to dominate and destroy,
maybe redemption for once being
a great country diced into a jigsaw puzzle,
partitioned now a fourth time,
crushed and enslaved by the Soviets
and Germans. Maybe someone
one rung lower was needed,
a sense of entitlement provoked.
Unlike the Nazis they weren't grandiose,
Empire Builders, just humble folk
seizing an opportunity to better themselves.
No one expected righteousness
from a serial killer, but the Zodiac
never claimed God was on his side.

14

Having been around philosophers so long
Betty knew better than to use logic
against obsession. It wasn't jealousy,
though she was jealous, but given
Heddie's résumé, she had reason
to be skeptical. It'd taken her two days
to hitchhike to my door from Berkeley,
an hour's trip, Betty reminded me,
because Heddie spent the night
with her first ride. She wondered
if my mother had ruined me for
adult women, or maybe I preferred
someone who didn't know who I was?
And who was that exactly? I asked.
Someone who blamed himself
for things he didn't do, an ex-Catholic
who still believed in crucifixion.

The day after Heddie moved in,
a drug dealer dropped by to tell me
she'd lived with him two months,
longer than with anyone else,
giving me maybe three weeks.
But the weeks passed, and then
the months. Maybe because I didn't ask
where she went or with whom.
I busied myself reading about Poland,
moving east into the past, which

seemed almost safer. About Swigge
she said: she liked him, but after
he proposed—yes, marriage—and
she refused, he cried all the time,
it was depressing. Sex was all Lou Phillips wanted.
When asked why she moved in with me,
she shrugged, smiled, and said:
"Sometimes you're cute
and even know things."

Why was I so smitten?
Her windswept, aquiline,
maverick ferocity? The languor
of her lanky unswerving faithlessness?

All I knew for sure was sometimes
it felt like driving around in circles
waiting for the Zodiac to end my misery.

15

Sometimes Mother confuses
her tenses, jumbles memories
of the slaughter with Chicago,
switching back and forth,
as if using the future to defend
herself against the past.
So that, near the end,

her dementia discloses
rather than obscures, her horror.
To render the excited faithfulness
of her desire to bear witness,
she gave up (and then I)
any attempt at precision,
or clarification.

. . . sometimes long ago is yesterday or a sleepless dream . . .
in Chicago is good but sometimes at the corner grocery
in the eyes of the grocer, a warm family man always smiling
I see . . . Jedwabne . . . laws and police here but if this man
could take someone's house . . . if a girl like Frumka he knew
all his life a sweet flower Henryk's age he could yank
from her father's arms and split in two like a leg of lamb
with an ax like Danil Kireyevich did always giving her
cookies in the dry goods store where he worked for
his uncle Popiolek and . . . Henryk's eyes seeing it . . .
will he remember . . . my neighbors here so different but . . .
Mr. Witherspoon upstairs coaches middle school basketball
picks and chooses some boys but not others making
the parents crazy . . . struts around a little king . . . under
his breath whispers blacks this women that—I recognize . . .
his eyes . . . to hate and want what isn't ours it's our nature . . .
but . . . Michal the blacksmith so excited to shove them inside
Sleszynski's barn and dose with kerosene he nails his hand
to the barn door . . . doesn't hear the children screaming . . .

I hear it . . . in my dreams . . . but Michal's deaf and dumb . . . and
Irena who helped me give birth to Henryk I beg make

her husband and brothers stop . . . the surprise in her eyes . . .
a stranger she's known all her life . . . a woman whose body
makes a child her ears can't hear a child being eaten by fire . . .
people Henryk knew running naked being hit with rakes and
pitchforks . . . beards on fire . . . infants clubbed . . . blood screaming
everywhere . . . after him all the way to Sleszynski's barn . . . I run
. . . on TV comedians making jokes about Jews blacks everyone
laughing . . . everything a joke . . . I clutch my rosaries praying for
dear Jesus Christ to come . . . "My soul is sorrowful until death . . ."
"their sins too He will take upon Himself . . . his sweat drops
of blood falling to the earth . . ."

a sunny morning 1961 but always 1941 . . . we moved town
to town . . . finally here to America . . . a new better life . . . baseball
movies Elvis Presley . . . but every cashier usher waiter mothers
wives . . . fathers . . . what hatred in their hearts . . . hidden . . .
a carnival everyone smiling drinking vodka . . . strangers . . .
Jews pleading for mercy . . . from people they thought they knew . . .
who went looking . . . for the sick the children they missed . . .

knocking with axes gold out of the teeth of corpses . . .
for rings fingers cut off . . . the Germans laughing . . . comedians . . .
making jokes . . . men with families, children the age of these . . .
only their own child is human . . . it's July the Germans yell
bury them or there'll be disease . . . kill too many and you
yourself will have to bury the bodies . . . the stink . . . in our hair
clothes . . . in Chicago people out in the spring streets . . . pushing
carriages . . . so proud of their families . . . happy to be alive . . .

"Hot Potato," the art of passing
the buck, Swigge'd called it.
A call transferred down here
this morning by someone anxious
to be rid of her. I'm the basement,
inactive files, I explain, she needs Medical . . .
"But they jus' transferred me here!"
"Believe me, I can't help you!"
"Mister—listen, I'm holding a knife
to my throat, I'm not kidding,
you'll be transferring a dead woman!"
I'm at my desk, eating lunch, dreaming
about Mexico, disappearing with Heddie.
Without another word, I should walk away,
up the stairs and out the front doors . . .
"Mister, you still there?"
"I am, yes. A knife?"
I'll never answer the phone again!
"I mean it, believe me!"
I nod, like an idiot.
"Say something!"
"What's your name, miss?"
"Zelda Progmeyer, with a P,
m-e-y-e-r, an old spelling,
you don't hear it anymore. Yours?"
"Henryk Wyrzykowski, also old."
"Polish? My first dead husband was,
as worthless as the second one."

I'm searching the directory for help,
trying to think. "Yes, Polish. Yours, English?"
"My mother was Irish, my father
from the land of drink and screaming.
When he finally noticed me
I was gone for ten years."
There's a city help line, Mrs. Cafiso
in Central Index would know what to do . . .
but she's out today, the Rev. Bingo
runs a work clinic for . . . "A maniac
plowed into my car, broke my back,
can't work with three kids they stopped
my disability, no one will tell me why!"
"Can you tell me your worker's name?
I'll stay on the line, talk to them . . ."
"Don't have one, missed too many appointments,
I need a special bed for my back,
maybe a new back, or life.
You can tell I'm serious, right?"
"Yes," I said. "Why like this,
on the phone with a stranger?"
"Misery loves company?"
Neither of us say anything.
"It's gets to a point where . . .
if it weren't for my kids . . ."
Swigge would've known what to do . . .
To distract her, I ask who transferred her.
"Somebody mean with a lisp,
must be your lucky day.
Last night I dreamed four guys

dressed like umpires buried me
alive in my backyard. Stripes and whistles—
whaddya make of that, mister?"
Staring into the stacks, listening
to her stifle tears, I decide to tell her
about Mother shooting my dog Buddy
because he wouldn't stop barking
at the hole people. "Sometimes
he comes back in dreams, always
happy to see me, all white except
for a black ring around his left eye."
"The color of grief," she says,
"what an awful dream, maybe
you should talk to someone . . ."
Now we're both laughing, slowly,
cautiously at first, then loudly,
without pausing for breath.
"You're too much!" she says,
and hangs up. A dial tone. Gone, fini,
Still holding the phone, listening
to our echoes, unable to move,
Yes, I think, the color of grief,
and begin laughing again.

Henryk, Himself Now

A Master of Sighs,

Is Discovered by the US Army,

and Takes Refuge Further Down

Inside

the Place Where Hell Is Made

I

About a month before Closed Files
and after teaching Spelling 1 & 2,
hoping to reinforce my ongoing argument
with my draft board, I went rollicking
over the countryside, with nine others
inside an old yellow school bus
over and around the lovely swaying hills
of Contra Costa County: two apoplectic SDS
higher-ups, one mostly blind ex-Black Panther
named Earl, a shivering lovely young
UC Berkeley dropout chemist named Jen,
a discombobulated army deserter,
two born-again ex-gangbangers socialists
from San Diego, one vodka-stinking
Methodist minister, two extra-large
black gospel singers on loan from
a traveling Baptist choir, one
Chicano Studies student writing
a thesis on the extinction of the Dodo bird,
all
on our way to replace the world-weary
at a New Year's Eve protest
at the Naval Munitions Depot
known as Port Chicago, where
all the napalm gets shipped from,
without compunction or regret.

Hoping we'll confront just a few lonely MPs
and not rowdy head-bashing townies
we're singing along with the driver's radio
to the Beatles' "I Am the Walrus"
the Methodist conducting,
the Baptist gospel singers goo-gooing
accompanied by the ex-Panther's congas
and a glistening flotilla of spit from
the Dodo bird guy's harmonica,
while outside the peaceful,
unsuspecting Contra Costa countryside
rolls and rambles by.

Reinforcements, or substitute ids
faking a beautiful rectitude
in order to slow the burning to a crisp
of the "commie gooks" readying themselves
to somehow attack us without an air force
or a single ship, all the while
welcoming in the New Year
at what our SDS guys call
"the Place where Hell is Made."

2

This morning in Central Index,
kidding with Mrs. Cafiso,
I was researching information

on a request for hearing aid batteries,
not a hearing aid but batteries,
made in Sacramento by a J.G. Frazer,
yes, the same name as
the Scottish anthropologist who imagined
the evolution of ancient myths, and wrote
The Golden Bough, dead since 1941
but now somehow in Sacramento requesting
hearing assistance. HHH still around,
or an inspired impostor? I was matching
ss numbers when a tall gangly clerk asked
if I knew a H.S. Wyrzykowki,
a name similar to mine but spelled differently.
In the bottom drawer of his new job's desk
he found this letter addressed to him,
dated five months ago.

Downstairs, where I belong,
my pulse a strong gale, 28–33 knots, I,
the same said H.S. Wyrzykowski
in order not to embrace as Swigge had done
the vast howling ocean wave of groveling pleas
everywhere around me and go bonkers,
I read the long-dormant letter
from my draft board, informing me
I've been tardy in all kinds of bad ways,
and therefore am now facing a jail term
of five years and/or a $5,000 penalty
unless I can prove I'm back in school
or ready to be a patriot.

3

Consider this: Suppose B says
he can no longer live inside
the dour language of his dreams,
which can't be quieted by drugs,
madness or divine fury.
Suppose, as Ludwig might,
over time the fear and humiliation
becomes so great his mind collapses in flames.
Suppose C says he can't surrender
any piece of his guilt for having survived
and must now repent by hesitating
indefinitely on the brink
of a profound ambivalence.
Suppose D can no longer mediate
the voices in his head to save himself.

Suppose D can't stop worrying
that his desire not to perish
reduced him to exactly the kind
of parasitic subspecies
his tormentors saw him as.

Suppose B realized
finally
that his wretchedness
wasn't original or prestigious,
that nothing ever would camouflage

the pornographic unctuousness
of his desire to exist.

Suppose D discovered
that he couldn't forgive the food
and valuables that he found inside
the train cars after a selection.
Not the corpses of children he disposed of,
or the vomit he swallowed afterwards
to not lose its nourishment,
its aftertaste of atonement.

Suppose B could stop despising himself
for getting used to everything,
even the souls of the dead
who speak to him in his dreams,
pleading for recompense,
and not to be forgotten.

Suppose that what B, C, and D
hated most of all was being told
when to stand, sit, eat and defecate,
what and when to speak, be awake,
not like children, but slaves building pyramids,
obstacles reduced to an idea, a number,
an object of such great abhorrence,
one becomes
finally
nothing more than a vacuum.

Suppose R,
being the son of such a man,
was the child of no one.

4

Betty, with a slight head shake,
can say: I told you so better than anyone.
She's doing it now, staring out
over our table window at
The Fish Factory in Ghirardelli Square,
looking without absorbing the splendors
of a clear summer Sunday,
the bridge hoisting itself high
on its own swagger, the submissive charms
of sailboats riding winds they seem startled by—
all splendid except for the shadow
cast by what I'm not saying:
hearing from my draft board,
because she'll tell me to run away.
Instead, I tell her about the guy
I found unconscious yesterday, slung
over my gas heater, gas everywhere.
Revived by coffee, compresses,
walking around, he came through
a back window, looking for Heddie,
he explained. Disconsolate,
the gas offered an end to his torment.

Asked, he said, no, he didn't wonder
how finding a strange corpse
in my living room might make me feel.
An out-of-work actor, he met her
making an adult film, which, yes,
she did, occasionally. The note
he planned to leave said:
I love you forever, Dwayne.
Betty, smiling now, prolongs
her silent treatment, which says:
Yes, but for the grace of God . . .
"Someone calls or comes by
almost every day," I say.
"She spent the weekend in Mendocino
with King Alphonso, a drug dealer
from the haunted streets of Guatemala."

All the pretty angling boats,
each lost in its own wake,
heading toward or away
from something maybe
a little less stupefying.

"Such a pretty place,
so much trouble,"
she finally says.

5

The draft got started under Truman,
the American Friends counselor
explains in his Powell Street office,
because peacetime conscription
was better than a volunteer army
which needs financial inducement.
Instead, they netted the uneducated
and minority poor as fodder.
I was lucky, mostly deferments
went to the privileged. "COs and 4-F
mentals are used up so unless
your ticker's bad sit it out in Canada,
lose your name and go underground,
or claim God and conscience and go to jail."
I asked what he would do. Go to Sweden,
he said, where war's outlawed
and the girls are pretty.
"We never spoke, good luck."

Back at work, swiveling,
my pulse 46 knots, I'm hoping
Mr. Piranesi, who probably knew
all about hiding, might now tell me
in his giant vaults, unsupportable balconies,
and menacing passages, under which
nothing lies but interminable darkness,
where I should go next. No city
or house divided against itself will stand,

Lincoln, by way of Christ, said.
Kill your own kind or die,
do nothing and go to jail . . .

Mother,
who hid others,
would choose jail, and honor,
or maybe suicide.
Betty says Canada.
Piranesi prefers the next level down,
where the light too hides.

6

To claim that Port Chicago
is the middle of nowhere
is at best a syllogism,
because it would imply
that nowhere also owns
a beginning and end.
Thus hell, which so many
in my files believe to be the end,
may actually be only a middle
or a beginning. Which is to say
that Port Chicago was not only
the middle of nowhere,
but also the beginning and end.

Behind
the barbed wire fence,
the bellicose apparatus: barracks,
radar towers, jeeps mounted
with machine guns, indolent soldiers
wandering in and out of a resourceful fog,
and across the highway two bored MPs
guarding a humongous gate through which,
infrequently, 18-wheelers—aka semi tractor
trailers big rig US transport trucks—pass,
carrying their dark cargo all the way
from somewhere to somewhere
in the vicinity of hell,
despite
our pitiable presence.

Indeed,
not the place in which
to welcome the New Year.
We sat shivering around a puny fire,
surrounded by foggy fields,
those we replaced long gone,
the Dodo bird guy perched in a juniper tree,
taking notes about us, I conjectured,
a species no less gone astray
than his favorite subject.
Asked by the chemist, Jen, why I'm here,
I say "To prove my insanity and feel less futile."
What I don't say is: having seen hell
many of the soldiers I taught

wanted to but didn't know how to look away.
Unable to speak about what they'd seen
their suffering continued.
I too wanted to look away,
be shaken loose.

Under
the minister's direction,
we're singing hymns, heads bowed
and hands joined. Earl
something bluesy, the gospels
more down-home, noises provocative
and strange—so, okay, eyes closed,
I'm saying hello to my Maker
with whom I haven't spoken for a while,
admitting foolishness,
ambitions too futile to avoid,
a kind of pouring forth of faith
into an ever more porous cup.

Until now
content to just pass by,
casting Evil Eyes, the caravan of townies stops.
Four souped-up black jalopy angels,
spitting dirt clouds,
blocking our view of the MPs,
sixteen doors emitting fifteen miscreants,
carrying bats, chains and tire irons.
"Go hide," I tell Jen, but it's too late,
already she's being looked over.

The Methodist imploring,
"Christ was born one week ago,
please boys, peace!"
"You commie faggots come all the way
out here looking for peace?"
a tall skinny blond boy says,
scraping the minister's chin with his knuckles.
"Brung your niggers too!"
"Hey, Bob, there's a pretty girl here!"
"I said No Names, moron!"

Everyone's scurrying back to their cars
as a cop pulls up and sticks
his head out of his headlights.
"I'd get out before they come back."
Our bus, the minister explains,
isn't due until noon the next day.

7

Some knew, the Survivor said,
where the trucks were taking them.
Trucks full of women and children
passing after a selection.
In their eyes and slumped bodies
even the ones who didn't know knew.
The resignation of the men staring
at the ground, not watching them pass

once, twice, five times a day, knew.
Wasn't it better for those
who didn't know not to?
Once he thought to cry out,
but didn't.

How ordinary it became.
How routine. Worst in spring
when to the trees life returns,
while in their souls winter remains.
If he could pray he'd pray to the god of death,
not depravity, desperation or cruelty, but death . . .
Who shall ascend the mountain of death . . .
I will lift up mine eyes to death . . .
the dead praise not the Lord . . .
valley of the shadow of death . . .
Our Father, our King Death . . .

Passing, on their way to be burned
and buried and dug up and buried again,
death already owned them.
Creatures so unbearable
they must be destroyed three times,
without anger, mercy,
or acknowledgment,
only death.

Yet
their faces remain,
too young and too old,

too pretty
and tired
and sick,
too lost in dreaming,
in the unknown,
passing and passing into anonymity
beyond which only time lives.

Did it matter why
they were so despised?
Why not once
did he or they cry out?

Because
they all already knew
everything had been lost?

8

Lisa,
a nurse in the Alzheimer's ward,
sent me a letter Mother wrote.

Dear Henryk,
My thoughts are leaving me . . .
So if you don't hear from me . . .
know I . . . didn't lose my faith but . . .
dignity . . . next to God I liked it best . . .

remember the blackberry wine
we made in the cellar, your tiny toes
all red and eyes alive with joy . . . I miss you
most dear boy . . . maybe because you
were forced to see such cruelty . . .
I couldn't cover your eyes . . . you kept
finding ways to look . . . I failed you
a hundred times . . . I tried but couldn't turn
my back on them . . . everyone, your father,
wanted me to . . . I was afraid all the time . . .
now everything is dark . . . after all that . . .
shouldn't there be light! . . . you've a good heart . . .
remember how you pounded your little fists
on our neighbors looking for gold they thought
the Jews gave us . . . how they beat me and you
pounded on them with your little fists and kicked . . .
one flung you by your hair against a stall . . .
I still want to rip their eyes out . . . me . . . a killer . . .
soon my mind will leave me . . . only night . . .
it makes me nervous . . . my hands shake
my mouth dries . . . our Jews are in Argentina,
send money . . . in God's eyes we're all one . . .
in God's eyes . . .

    all my love,
    Antonia

9

Daybreak
like so much algae spills
all over my one good and one
swollen shut left eye.
No one ambitious enough to rebuild the dead fire.
Meanwhile, Jen, behind the Dodo's juniper,
sobbing in the minister's arms.
Everyone speaking to himself.
Like an evil dream the thugs
quickly came and went, leaving us
beaten, robbed and dispirited.
Across the highway,
new MPs are staring at us,
curious perhaps about the weeping.
The ones they replaced ignored our cries.
We were asking for it, their expression said.

Indeed,
the Piper was paid in blood.

The gospel singers look dazed,
not half a hymn left in them.
Jen, traumatized, can't stop crying.
But the fog is lifting, sunlight awaking the hills,
the moon taking its leaving slow,
curious perhaps what might become of us.

Having busted my jaw,
kicked Earl in the eye,
the blond thug, upon leaving, said,
"Maybe you learned something . . ."

Yes, maybe something was learned,
though I can't say what exactly.

Maybe
the Dodoist, high in his juniper,
cawing,
knows.

Not one word of welcome
from any of us
to this brand new
New Year.

10

Swigge,
based on this last entry,
tired of the disenchantment
of the atavistic testimony surrounding him,
finally, I imagine, had enough
and decided to be somewhere else,
to leave this place.

"Upstairs they're investigating me,
Heddie or husbanding Hoeckstra's
resourcefulness, abetting and promoting
what genius a place like this is capable of . . .
it no longer matters. Lou Phillips has reason
to want me gone. Jesus thought humility
beautiful, the poor the first through
heaven's gates. On some level, yes,
a comedy, crumbs tossed, gratitude
expected. Me, a clean shirt passing
in the halls, privy to a party they're
not invited to . . . how I envy them no longer
having to pretend to be what they're not,
they know their suffering sustains us,
validates our importance, that without
them our happiness is impossible. Pity
the most powerful aphrodisiac, pity
and disgust. They've been here since
the beginning of time, waiting to serve us.
Our sob to Cerberus, sacrifice to fate.
Maybe I'm crazy but when I look under
the dirt and foul stink I see the remains
of my humanity. What lies crushed
and wasted in me, under all the brine
and sacrilege, all the fear and pretense—
the remains of what's good in me.
They're everything we're afraid of,
alone and cornered, spoiled possibility,
defeated dreams . . . belittled, cajoled,

ignored, abandoned . . . here, in the midst
of such great abundance without doubt
they're our last chance . . ."

11

Once,
after the Survivor
screamed in his sleep
about having to sweep and clean
and bury mountains of ash,
Rossy took out of our library
a book about cremation to learn
what it consisted of, and said:
"It's hard to follow: If analyzed by X-ray,
using something called photoelectron
spectroscopy, or quantitative
spectroscopic techniques that measure
a material's elemental composition,
incinerated organic matter,
a human body, basically, undergoes
tremendous change, reduced
to mineral residue siliceous aggregates
make up a large proportion of
the highly unstable remains,
called cremains, which, given
changes in climate, geology and ecology

over millennia, become pulverized
particulate matter making up about
3.5 percent of the body's original mass,
which makes good fertilizer
(calcium phosphate occurring
naturally in cow milk); out of which
the only chemical components left
are the non-burnable elements,
bones and teeth, dental and surgical
prostheses . . . and so on . . ."

In other words,
at the age of twelve,
Rossy tried to understand
a process explanation couldn't explain.
He, I, understood nothing
about a transformation so deliberate,
so thought-through, predetermined,
it came to represent
the human body's final function.
After so much thought and feeling,
so many memories and desires,
transformed and modified
finally to ash.

Yes,
a Torah of sorts,
of endless stories,
analysis, rules
and afterthoughts.

12

Milt had studied Plato
with Betty's ex-husband
but now helped guys like me
disappear into Mexico.
She took me to Oakland to see him.
It was simple, he said,
his contacts in Taos, Mazatlán
and Guadalajara would help me find work,
a new identity, and a place to stay
so after a year, when I was twenty-six
and no longer draft eligible,
when most likely there'd be
some kind of amnesty, I could return.
Mexico was easier, cheaper
and less obvious than Canada.
I had to leave without telling anyone
where, or giving notice at work.
Just disappear, Milt said, in a week or ten days.
It'll get lonely and weird, but plenty
others were in my situation,
I just had to go. Quickly and quietly.

Later, at the bay, watching boats
bob past, tourists hurrying
toward the next view, the next decision,
one of Ludwig's signals
seemed to be beckoning me
from my hiding place. Mexico

seemed so innocent and antique.
Maybe finally,
and once again,
it was time to change.

Outside,
flocks of dithering seagulls
scanning the waves,
everything so settled,
so completely up in the air.

13

With letters, phone calls and cryptograms,
the Zodiac expressed his desire
for a slave colony in paradise.
Paradise in the cosmogonical,
or eschatological sense, being one
of the last four events of history,
the others being: death, judgment, and hell.
A "higher place" being positive,
harmonious and timeless, in contrast
to the suffering on earth and below.
An abode of the virtuous dead.
In the Gospel of Luke Jesus tells
a penitent criminal being crucified
next to him, that they'll be together
in paradise. In old Egyptian beliefs,

it's an otherworld of fields ideal
for hunting and fishing, where
the dead live after judgment.
The Greeks have their Elysian fields,
a land of plenty in which the heroic
and righteous spend eternity.
The Vedic Indians cremate the body
so the soul in the Third Heaven
can know bliss. The Hebrew paradise
is a garden where Adam's body
was carried by the archangel Michael.
A mystical place, where, the Zohar says:
peshat (literal meaning), remez (allusion),
derash (anagogical) and sod (mystical)
form the initials of the word P(a) rd (e) s,
representing, in biblical exegesis,
the fourfold interpretation of the Torah.

In none
a place to imprison slaves.

Perhaps
in trying to define paradise
Hitler and the Zodiac
confused it with hell,
each devising a unique
and ingenuous place
in which the dead await
a judgment that never arrives.

14

Hurrying home from work
to ask Heddie to come to Mexico with me,
I found this note on my refrigerator,
taped to a pressed flower.

Dear Henry,
I warned you I was a bird of passage,
always going somewhere else.
Now Taos. The wildflower is a yellow
evening star my dad gave me before
he left for good when I was ten. Just
a common field flower, like me I guess.
You're a good home for it. I know you
care for me but I don't know why.

        Heddie

Maybe it was for the best.
At least now I knew she loved me,
in her way.

15

Mother's last diaries,
numbers 21 & 22, though vivid,
confuse things she didn't see

but overheard and was later told,
with things she saw firsthand,
details and sentences collapsing
under the weight of her grief
and disbelief. In her delirium,
and in mine, scenes unfold
with the force of a living chronicle.

One additional thing,
in order to align my consciousness
with her dementia,
I dropped a tablet of acid:

. . . so many murderers coming from other towns . . .
from Radzilow and Wasosz . . . killing and plundering
rounding Jews up to burn in Sleszynski's barn . . .
down the street kicked like cattle to the Jewish
cemetery across the square . . . where the brute
Kobrzyniecki was boasting 18 he killed like cows
and pigs . . . pulling Henryk away the kheyder teacher's
daughter Gitele Nadolny a girl always so good
to Henryk now knocked to the ground and kicked . . .
a scythe sent her head flying like a pumpkin . . .
her blue eyes still so big . . . a girl so beautiful
her father cried to gaze upon her . . . great laughing
and clapping . . . at such a sight . . . covering Henryk's eyes
. . . pulling away, bawling . . . everyone rushing toward
Sleszynski's barn . . . covering their heads genitals
the Jews pushed punched and kicked from every side . . .
a river of burning sunlight . . . rushing . . . toward . . .

Jumbled,
too frenzied
to harness or identify,
words are hopping
and skipping over
the pages of her diary . . .
some bursting into flames,
scorching my thumbs . . .
the word *road* kicking
and punching the word *down*
in its genitals
leaping from Polish
to Yiddish
and back into Polish
wanting nothing to do
with English with Ludwig
who's telling everyone
he's a Catholic not a Jew
not a Pole just feeding
his stupid cattle more
spoiled language as if
it'll make them think
about what they're doing,
the wild blue ether
of his meaning
as butchered as ever . . .

. . . my eyes are burning . . . God in heaven . . . Matthew said
"But I say unto you, that whosoever is angry with his brother
without cause shall be in danger of the judgment . . . of hell fire" . . .

even the clouds are fleeing . . . a child's beautiful head cut off . . .
farmers growing seeds of death for Satan to reap . . .

Rossy jumping off
the reservoir's edge
into the warm spring day
we're playing hooky
dunking each other deep
under the sunlight
where the singing is . . .
like us God is fourteen . . .
the files everywhere burning
woeful inky snake words
slithering
out of the shadows
pleas erupting
out of yellowing pages
bent paper clips
attacking rusted staples
strutting about taking photos
to show off back at home—
pity-engorged histories
fleeing the heat . . .
O my God!—Rossy
deep under
the dark water,
so far down
far away . . .

. . . God's tears raining down . . . as if they're not like us
with hands eyes and hearts pumping blood . . . lustful beasts
insane for property . . . the lowly Jews a little better off
better heads for business . . . the devil's revenge . . . everyone
needs someone to kick . . .

here too—devils!
breaking free leaping
over the files
eating entire cases
drinking gallons of inky woe
joining hands dancing jigs
sprinkling a spoiled joy
over
the inactive cases
whirling dervishes
kicking high
over
the listless shadows
all my pathetic darlings . . .

now . . . too late to get away to run . . . the fields the sky
the trees the barns . . . nowhere to run . . . the trees looking away . . .
push them inside Sleszynski's barn . . . a few trying to run . . .
into the cemetery . . . hide in fields . . . crows pecking clawing
at strong boys their legs arms tongues torn out . . . the sky
red as Satan . . . doors slamming shut . . . a deluge of kerosene
. . . a black glee . . .

. . . tunnels 23 feet deep
50 sq. miles wide
arcs of fire hot tamales
thought logs banging end to end—
a cauldron of camouflage
hopping over rice paddies
the remote Vu Quang reserve
another Javan rhino on the run
trying to avoid being butchered
bursting into flames
Ho Chi himself calling me
inside slamming doors . . .
to say so long goodbye
dear Giovanni Batista Piranesi
hiding deep
in his basement
another tunnel rat
scurrying in and out of
scorched shadows
out
of this melting jungle . . .

. . . deeper inside . . . doors windows living people . . .
eyes turning into torches . . . beasts not slaughtered
like this . . . dear sweet Jesus crying "Hell: where
the worm dieth not and the fire is not quenched . . .
the worm and maggots never lacked to eat—
always alive always in existence . . ." devils now
outside dancing as inside women and infants howl
arms raised to the Lord . . .

Oh Lord the screaming . . . scorching God's ears . . .

please dear lord in heaven—hear this
listen to this . . .

. . . the banging tearing at wood nails at flesh . . .
mercy nailed shut . . . to its cross . . . no pity . . . no
understanding that God too sees this . . .

Up on my desk now
standing on one leg
tasting
the air's temperature
in heaven
in hell
with a finger I don't recognize
balancing on one leg
like a crane
flames leaping
from my shoes crawling
up my pants worms snakes tongues of flames
on one leg
hearing the screaming inside the files
all the woe being eaten alive
all the brilliant schemes to survive . . .
wasted . . .

. . . inside flames burrowing deeper planks collapsing
. . . what . . . one last breath . . . for merciful darkness . . .
last drop of light . . . oh solemn grace . . . garbage dump

of the valley of Hen . . . maggots and worms will go hungry
nothing left to feast on . . . the trees of heaven burning . . .

napalm raining over every file
every case history a jungle
of falling blackness
a raging black river of fire
I'm going to Vietnam
to the jungles of Khe Sanh
to hide from
the ever shifting tides of desire
rising price of staying alive
all the melting bodies
crushed
asphyxiated
buried and dug up
searched for
one last gold coin
everything alive
burning . . .

. . . the flames climbing my legs too my arms eating
my heart black the light the fire lifting me in its great wings
high above the barn up into the sky higher and higher
Henryk in my arms his dear sweet eyes wondering
where we're going . . . with all the other souls lifting
their beautiful wings of fire the sky filled with souls
rising higher than the harm higher than evil . . . all of us
now rising up into His . . . merciful arms . . .

16

Yes,
what we do with our lives.
Suffering is useful.
Even necessary and brilliant,
especially
when every sign seems dead.

These last hours of work seem no longer mine.
Here a short while and then gone,
some noisy moments of serenity,
quiet triumph, then once again the silence
of being somewhere in-between.

The blond thug's words echo all the way
from Port Chicago to down here:
maybe you learned something . . . Yes,
but what? A refrain as well as a dictum,
what did and didn't occur and to whom?
I know now that Mother is perhaps
the happiest person alive.
She didn't turn away, but stood there,
eyes wide open, seeing everything.
Her suffering was useful, it helped her
stand up to her fear. I also didn't, finally,
turn away. What I learned about myself
is limited to what I know about human beings.
That we're despicable and unworthy
and sometimes magnanimous enough
to survive with dignity.

The unspeakable things we do,
the vicious lies we tell ourselves and others,
the innocence we beat to death
with and without shame, is always there
in the smallest gesture of our eyes
and hands and tongues. There
in the only wealth and meaning
we possess, the fragile filament
of our humanity, which perhaps
is what we envy and suspect and fear
and want to kill in others.
Without it there is nothing
but infinite black space,
ripples on a lake, screams no one hears.
Is this why we speak and listen,
suffer grief and fear,
and seek forgiveness
even while living in a hole?

Such stately and curious specimens,
so many ghostly echoes.
Goodbye Henryk Wyrzykowski,
and all the still rising souls
of Jedwabne—listen

off
the pitiless cinderblock
everywhere
the softest, tiniest echoing:

Yitgadal veyitkadash

shemei raba

bealma divera chireutei

veyamlich malchutei

bechayeichon uveyomeichon

uvechayei dechol beit Yisraeil

baagala uvizeman kariv,

veimeru: amein . . .

The End

Acknowledgments

Sections of this poem previously appeared in *The New York Times*, to whose editors grateful acknowledgment is made.

I drew inspiration, courage, and invaluable information from the following books: Saul Friedländer's monumental *The Years of Extermination: Nazi Germany and the Jews, 1939–1945* (HarperCollins, 2007) and *The Years of Persecution, 1933–1939* (HarperCollins, 1997); Jan T. Gross's *Neighbors*—a book that inspired my own—(Princeton University Press, 2001), *Fear* (Random House, 2006), and *Golden Harvest* (Oxford University Press, 2012); Elie Wiesel, *Night*, *Dawn*, and *Day* (Hill & Wang, 2006); Christopher R. Browning's *Ordinary Men* (HarperCollins, 1992) and *Remembering Survival* (W. W. Norton, 2010); Yehuda Bauer's *The Death of the Shtetl* (Yale University Press, 2009) and *Rethinking the Holocaust* (Yale University Press, 2001); Raul Hilberg, *The Destruction of the European Jews* (Yale University Press, 2003); *Voices & Views: A History of the Holocaust*, edited with an introduction by Deborah Dwork (The Jewish Foundation for the Righteous, 2002); Timothy Snyder, *Bloodlands* (Basic Books, 2010); Aharon Appelfeld, *The Story of a Life* (Schocken Books, 2004) and *Badenheim 1939* (David R. Godine, 2009); *The Last Jew of Treblinka*, a memoir by Chil Rajchman (Pegasus Books, 2009); Art Spiegelman, *Maus I & II: A Survivor's Tale* (Pantheon Books, 1986 and 1991); Primo Levi, *Survival in Auschwitz* (Macmillan, 1961), *The Reawakening* (Macmillan, 1965), and *The Drowned and the Saved* (Summit Books, 1986); Charles Reznikoff, *Holocaust* (Black Sparrow Press and David R. Godine, 2007); Anne Frank, *The Diary of a Young Girl* (Peguin, 2001); Tadeusz Borowski, *This Way for the Gas, Ladies and Gentlemen* (Penguin, 1976); Heimrad Backer, *transcript* (Dalkey Archive, 2010); Hans Keilson, *Comedy in a Minor Key* and *The Death of the Adversary* (Farrar, Straus &

Giroux, 2010); Imre Kertész, *Fateless* (Northwestern University Press, 1992); Adam Michnik, *In Search of Lost Meaning* (University of California Press, 2011); Mark Gerzon, *The Whole World Is Watching* (Paperback Library, 1970); Michael Harrington, *The Other America: Poverty in the United States* (Penguin, 1971); Jiří Weil, *Life with a Star* (Farrar, Straus & Giroux, 1989); Howard Morley Sachar, *The Course of Modern Jewish History* (Dell, 1958); Gerald Howard, editor, *The Sixties* (Pocket Books, 1982); Morris Dickstein, *Gates of Eden* (Basic Books, 1977); American Friends Service Committee, *The Draft?* (Hill & Wang, 1968); New York State Department of Social Services, *What You Should Know About Your Rights and Responsibilities*; Ivan T. Vassey, *Developing a Data Storage and Retrieval System* (Social Casework #49, Onondaga County Child Guidance Center, 1968); Frances Fox Piven and Richard A. Cloward, *Regulating the Poor: The Functions of Public Welfare* (Vintage, 1971); Frantz Fanon, *The Wretched of the Earth* (Grove Press, 1963); and special gratitude and admiration to Ludwig Wittgenstein's *Philosophical Investigations*, translated by G.E.M. Anscombe (Macmillan, 1968).

I want to thank those good souls who provided guidance and succor: Lawrence Besserman, Carl Dennis, Lesley Dormen, Newman Fisher, Saul Friedländer, Marc Frons, Nancy Green, Jan T. Gross, Sigmund Heuberg, James Lasdun, Paul Muldoon, Grace Schulman, Rosanna Warren, Cynthia Weiner, and Rabbi Sheldon Zimmerman. Gratitude also to Drenka Willen and Georges Borchardt, there from the beginning, and to my editor, Jill Bialosky, a wise and patient guardian angel, and to my sons, Eli and Augie, who provided the gift of joy during this long journey, and to my wife, Monica Banks, whose own wherewithal served as both example and revelation.

Notes

Ampère's Law, on page 37, is a law of classical electromagnetism discovered by André-Marie Ampère in 1826, describing the integrated magnetic field and a closed loop to the electric current passing through the loop.

The History of the English Poor Laws, on page 44, refers to the Poor Law Amendment Act of 1834, known as the New Poor Law, passed by the Whig government of Earl Grey that reformed the country's poverty relief system. The PLAA curbed the cost of poor relief, which had been spiraling throughout the nineteenth century, and led to the creation of workhouses.

The quote beginning section 16 on page 51 and the quotes from Karl Marx are from *Voices & Views, A History of the Holocaust*, edited by Deborah Dwork, The Jewish Foundation for the Righteous, 2002.

The Ku Klux Klan quote on page 70 is taken from *The Draft*, from the Peace Education Division of the American Friends Service Committee (page 21, W. Walker, *The Veteran Comes Back*, New York, Dryden Press, 1944).

The Michael Harrington quote that begins section 10 on page 70 is from his essay "The Two Nations" from *The Other America*.

The Zodiac killer's letter on page 74 is from the *San Francisco Examiner*, August 7, 1969, sent in response to Chief Stiltz's request for more details to prove he killed people he claimed to. This is the first time the killer used this name for identification.

"I like killing people Because . . ." on page 101 is from a letter the Zodiac killer sent to the *Vallejo Times Herald*, the *San Francisco Chronicle*, and the *San Francisco Examiner*, on August 1, 1969, a 408-symbol cryptogram in which he claimed his identity.